DATE DUE

GAYLORD

PRINTED IN U.S.A.

D1442962

THE HISTORY & CULTURE of NATIVE AMERICANS

The

Hopi

ᴛʜᴇHISTORY & CULTURE of NATIVE AMERICANS

The Apache

The Blackfeet

The Cherokee

The Cheyenne

The Choctaw

The Comanche

The Hopi

The Iroquois

The Lakota Sioux

The Mohawk

The Navajo

The Nez Perce

The Seminole

The Zuni

THE HISTORY & CULTURE of NATIVE AMERICANS

The Hopi

BARRY PRITZKER

Series Editor
PAUL C. ROSIER

CHELSEA HOUSE
An Infobase Learning Company

The Hopi

Chelsea House
An imprint of Infobase Learning
132 West 31st Street
New York, NY 10001

Library of Congress Cataloging-in-Publication Data

Pritzker, Barry.
  The Hopi / Barry Pritzker.
    p. cm. — (The history and culture of Native Americans)
  Includes bibliographical references and index.
    ISBN 978-1-60413-798-9 (hardcover : alk. paper)   1. Hopi Indians—History—
Juvenile literature.   2. Hopi Indians—Social life and customs—Juvenile literature.
I. Title.   II. Series.

  E99.H7P74 2011
  979.1004'97485—dc22

                                                                              2010052645

Chelsea House books are available at special discounts when purchased in bulk quantities for businesses, associations, institutions, or sales promotions. Please call our Special Sales Department in New York at (212) 967-8800 or (800) 322-8755.

You can find Chelsea House on the World Wide Web at
http://www.infobaselearning.com

Text design by Lina Farinella
Cover design by Alicia Post
Composition by Newgen North America
Cover printed by Yurchak Printing, Landisville, Pa.
Book printed and bound by Yurchak Printing, Landisville, Pa.
Date printed: May 2011
Printed in the United States of America

10 9 8 7 6 5 4 3 2 1

This book is printed on acid-free paper.

All links and Web addresses were checked and verified to be correct at the time of publication. Because of the dynamic nature of the Web, some addresses and links may have changed since publication and may no longer be valid.

Contents

Foreword

by Paul C. Rosier

Native American words, phrases, and tribal names are embedded in the very geography of the United States—in the names of creeks, rivers, lakes, cities, and states, including Alabama, Connecticut, Iowa, Kansas, Illinois, Missouri, Oklahoma, and many others. Yet Native Americans remain the most misunderstood ethnic group in the United States. This is a result of limited coverage of Native American history in middle schools, high schools, and colleges; poor coverage of contemporary Native American issues in the news media; and stereotypes created by Hollywood movies, sporting events, and TV shows.

Two newspaper articles about American Indians caught my eye in recent months. Paired together, they provide us with a good introduction to the experiences of American Indians today: first, how they are stereotyped and turned into commodities; and second, how they see themselves being a part of the United States and of the wider world. (Note: I use the terms *Native Americans* and *American Indians* interchangeably; both terms are considered appropriate.)

In the first article, "Humorous Souvenirs to Some, Offensive Stereotypes to Others," written by Carol Berry in *Indian Country Today,* I read that tourist shops in Colorado were selling "souvenir" T-shirts portraying American Indians as drunks. "My Indian name is Runs with Beer," read one T-shirt offered in Denver. According to the article, the T-shirts are "the kind of stereotype-reinforcing products also seen in nearby Boulder, Estes Park, and likely other Colorado communities, whether as part of the tourism trade or as everyday merchandise." No other ethnic group in the United States is stereotyped in such a public fashion. In addition, Native people are used to sell a range of consumer goods, including the Jeep Cherokee, Red Man chewing tobacco, Land O'Lakes butter, and other items that either objectify or insult them, such as cigar store Indians. As importantly, non-Indians learn about American Indian history and culture through sports teams such as the Atlanta Braves, Cleveland Indians, Florida State Seminoles, or Washington Redskins, whose name many American Indians consider a racist insult; dictionaries define *redskin* as a "disparaging" or "offensive" term for American Indians. When fans in Atlanta do their "tomahawk chant" at Braves baseball games, they perform two inappropriate and related acts: One, they perpetuate a stereotype of American Indians as violent; and two, they tell a historical narrative that covers up the violent ways that Georgians treated the Cherokee during the Removal period of the 1830s.

The second article, written by Melissa Pinion-Whitt of the San Bernardino *Sun* addressed an important but unknown dimension of Native American societies that runs counter to the irresponsible and violent image created by products and sporting events. The article, "San Manuels Donate $1.7 M for Aid to Haiti," described a Native American community that had sent aid to Haiti after it was devastated in January 2010 by an earthquake that killed more than 200,000 people, injured hundreds of thousands more, and destroyed the Haitian capital. The San Manuel Band of Mission Indians in California donated $1.7 million to help relief efforts in Haiti; San Manuel children held fund-raisers to collect additional donations. For the San Manuel Indians it was nothing new; in 2007 they had donated $1 million to help Sudanese refugees in Darfur. San Manuel also contributed $700,000 to relief efforts following Hurricane Katrina and Hurricane Rita, and donated $1 million in 2007 for wildfire recovery in Southern California.

Such generosity is consistent with many American Indian nations' cultural practices, such as the "give-away," in which wealthy tribal members give to the needy, and the "potlatch," a winter gift-giving ceremony and feast tradition shared by tribes in the

Pacific Northwest. And it is consistent with historical accounts of American Indians' generosity. For example, in 1847 Cherokee and Choctaw, who had recently survived their forced march on a "Trail of Tears" from their homelands in the American South to present-day Oklahoma, sent aid to Irish families after reading of the potato famine, which created a similar forced migration of Irish. A Cherokee newspaper editorial, quoted in Christine Kinealy's *The Great Irish Famine: Impact, Ideology, and Rebellion,* explained that the Cherokee "will be richly repaid by the consciousness of having done a good act, by the moral effect it will produce abroad." During and after World War II, nine Pueblo communities in New Mexico offered to donate food to the hungry in Europe, after Pueblo army veterans told stories of suffering they had witnessed while serving in the United States armed forces overseas. Considering themselves a part of the wider world, Native people have reached beyond their borders, despite their own material poverty, to help create a peaceful world community.

American Indian nations have demonstrated such generosity within the United States, especially in recent years. After the terrorist attacks of September 11, 2001, the Lakota Sioux in South Dakota offered police officers and emergency medical personnel to New York City to help with relief efforts; Indian nations across the country sent millions of dollars to help the victims of the attacks. As an editorial in the *Native American Times* newspaper explained on September 12, 2001, "American Indians love this country like no other. . . . Today, we are all New Yorkers."

Indeed, Native Americans have sacrificed their lives in defending the United States from its enemies in order to maintain their right to be both American and Indian. As the volumes in this series tell us, Native Americans patriotically served as soldiers (including as "code talkers") during World War I and World War II, as well as during the Korean War, the Vietnam War, and, after 9/11, the wars in Afghanistan and Iraq. Native soldiers, men and women, do so today by the tens of thousands because they believe in America, an

America that celebrates different cultures and peoples. Sgt. Leonard Gouge, a Muscogee Creek, explained it best in an article in *Cherokee News Path* in discussing his post-9/11 army service. He said he was willing to serve his country abroad because "by supporting the American way of life, I am preserving the Indian way of life."

This new Chelsea House series has two main goals. The first is to document the rich diversity of American Indian societies and the ways their cultural practices and traditions have evolved over time. The second goal is to provide the reader with coverage of the complex relationships that have developed between non-Indians and Indians over the past several hundred years. This history helps to explain why American Indians consider themselves both American and Indian and why they see preserving this identity as a strength of the American way of life, as evidence to the rest of the world that America is a champion of cultural diversity and religious freedom. By exploring Native Americans' cultural diversity and their contributions to the making of the United States, these volumes confront the stereotypes that paint all American Indians as the same and portray them as violent; as "drunks," as those Colorado T-shirts do; or as rich casino owners, as many news accounts do.

* * *

Each of the 14 volumes in this series is written by a scholar who shares my conviction that young adult readers are both fascinated by Native American history and culture and have not been provided with sufficient material to properly understand the diverse nature of this complex history and culture. The authors themselves represent a varied group that includes university teachers and professional writers, men and women, and Native and non-Native. To tell these fascinating stories, this talented group of scholars has examined an incredible variety of sources, both the primary sources that historical actors have created and the secondary sources that historians and anthropologists have written to make sense of the past.

Although the 14 Indian nations (also called tribes and communities) selected for this series have different histories and cultures, they all share certain common experiences. In particular, they had to face an American empire that spread westward in the eighteenth and nineteenth centuries, causing great trauma and change for all Native people in the process. Because each volume documents American Indians' experiences dealing with powerful non-Indian institutions and ideas, I outline below the major periods and features of federal Indian policy making in order to provide a frame of reference for complex processes of change with which American Indians had to contend. These periods—Assimilation, Indian New Deal, Termination, Red Power, and Self-determination—and specific acts of legislation that define them—in particular the General Allotment Act, the Indian Reorganization Act, and the Indian Self-determination and Education Assistance Act—will appear in all the volumes, especially in the latter chapters.

In 1851, the commissioner of the federal Bureau of Indian Affairs (BIA) outlined a three-part program for subduing American Indians militarily and assimilating them into the United States: concentration, domestication, and incorporation. In the first phase, the federal government waged war with the American Indian nations of the American West in order to "concentrate" them on reservations, away from expanding settlements of white Americans and immigrants. Some American Indian nations experienced terrible violence in resisting federal troops and state militia; others submitted peacefully and accepted life on a reservation. During this phase, roughly from the 1850s to the 1880s, the U.S. government signed hundreds of treaties with defeated American Indian nations. These treaties "reserved" to these American Indian nations specific territory as well as the use of natural resources. And they provided funding for the next phase of "domestication."

During the domestication phase, roughly the 1870s to the early 1900s, federal officials sought to remake American Indians in the mold of white Americans. Through the Civilization Program, which actually started with President Thomas Jefferson, federal officials sent religious missionaries, farm instructors, and teachers to the newly created reservations in an effort to "kill the Indian to save the man," to use a phrase of that time. The ultimate goal was to extinguish American Indian cultural traditions and turn American Indians into Christian yeoman farmers. The most important piece of legislation in this period was the General Allotment Act (or Dawes Act), which mandated that American Indian nations sell much of their territory to white farmers and use the proceeds to farm on what was left of their homelands. The program was a failure, for the most part, because white farmers got much of the best arable land in the process. Another important part of the domestication agenda was the federal boarding school program, which required all American Indian children to attend schools to further their rejection of Indian ways and the adoption of non-Indian ways. The goal of federal reformers, in sum, was to incorporate (or assimilate) American Indians into American society as individual citizens and not as groups with special traditions and religious practices.

During the 1930s some federal officials came to believe that American Indians deserved the right to practice their own religion and sustain their identity as Indians, arguing that such diversity made America stronger. During the Indian New Deal period of the 1930s, BIA commissioner John Collier devised the Indian Reorganization Act (IRA), which passed in 1934, to give American Indian nations more power, not less. Not all American Indians supported the IRA, but most did. They were eager to improve their reservations, which suffered from tremendous poverty that resulted in large measure from federal policies such as the General Allotment Act.

Some federal officials opposed the IRA, however, and pushed for the assimilation of American Indians in a movement called Termination. The two main goals of Termination advocates, during the 1950s and 1960s, were to end (terminate) the federal reservation system and American Indians' political sovereignty derived from treaties and to relocate American Indians from rural reservations to urban areas. These coercive federal assimilation policies in turn generated resistance from Native Americans, including young activists who helped to create the so-called Red Power era of the 1960s and 1970s, which coincided with the African-American civil rights movement. This resistance led to the federal government's rejection of Termination policies in 1970. And in 1975 the U.S. Congress passed the Indian Self-determination and Education Assistance Act, which made it the government's policy to support American Indians' right to determine the future of their communities. Congress then passed legislation to help American Indian nations to improve reservation life; these acts strengthened American Indians' religious freedom, political sovereignty, and economic opportunity.

All American Indians, especially those in the western United States, were affected in some way by the various federal policies described above. But it is important to highlight the fact that each American Indian community responded in different ways to these pressures for change, both the detribalization policies of assimilation and the retribalization policies of self-determination. There is no one group of "Indians." American Indians were and still are a very diverse group. Some embraced the assimilation programs of the federal government and rejected the old traditions; others refused to adopt non-Indian customs or did so selectively, on their own terms. Most American Indians, as I noted above, maintain a dual identity of American and Indian.

Today, there are more than 550 American Indian (and Alaska Natives) nations recognized by the federal government. They have a legal and political status similar to states, but they have special rights and privileges that are the result of congressional acts and the hundreds of treaties that still govern federal-Indian relations today. In July 2008, the total population of American Indians (and Alaska Natives) was 4.9 million, representing about 1.6 percent of the United States population. The state with the highest number of American Indians is California, followed by Oklahoma, home to the Cherokee (the largest American Indian nation in terms of population), and then Arizona, home to the Navajo (the second-largest American Indian nation). All told, roughly half of the American Indian population lives in urban areas; the other half lives on reservations and in other rural parts of the country. Like all their fellow American citizens, American Indians pay federal taxes, obey federal laws, and vote in federal, state, and local elections; they also participate in the democratic processes of their American Indian nations, electing judges, politicians, and other civic officials.

This series on the history and culture of Native Americans celebrates their diversity and differences as well as the ways they have strengthened the broader community of America. Ronnie Lupe, the chairman of the White Mountain Apache government in Arizona, once addressed questions from non-Indians as to "why Indians serve the United States with such distinction and honor?" Lupe, a Korean War veteran, answered those questions during the Gulf War of 1991–1992, in which Native American soldiers served to protect the independence of the Kuwaiti people. He explained in "Chairman's Corner" in *The Fort Apache Scout* that "our loyalty to the United States goes beyond our need to defend our home and reservation lands. . . . Only a few in this country really understand that the indigenous people are a national treasure. Our values have the potential of creating the social, environmental, and spiritual healing that could make this country truly great."

—Paul C. Rosier
Associate Professor of History
Villanova University

Origins to 1540

The Hopi Indians are the westernmost of the Pueblo peoples. Their language, also called Hopi, is a Shoshonean language, which is a member of the Uto-Aztecan language family. The name "Hopi" comes from *Hopituh Shi-nu-mu*, which means "Peaceful People" or "People Who Live in the Correct Way." (The Hopi used to be known as "Moki" or "Moqui," an uncomplimentary name that probably came from their Zuni neighbors.) Hopi land is located on the Colorado Plateau, north and east of the Little Colorado River, and especially at the southern tip of Black Mesa, on three high mesas (known as First Mesa, Second Mesa, and Third Mesa) that extend into the dry, high plain below, in what is now northeastern Arizona. Prehistoric Hopi were part of a culture group sometimes known as Anasazi. Since the word "Anasazi" comes from a Navajo word that means "enemy ancestors," many Pueblo people consider it to be offensive and now use the term Ancestral Puebloan to describe their forebears.

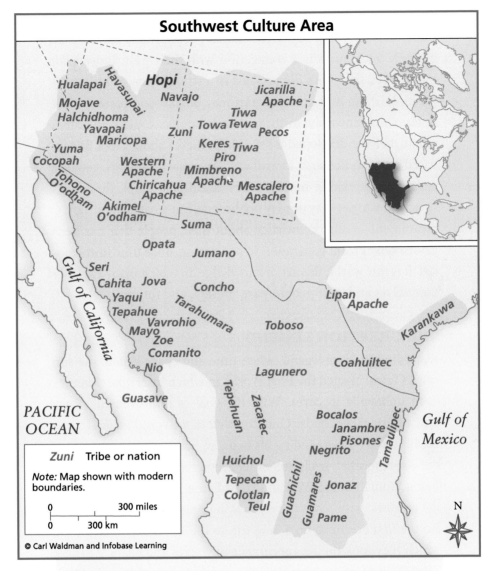

Southwest Culture Area

Hualapai
Havasupai
Hopi
Navajo
Jicarilla Apache
Mojave
Halchidhoma
Yavapai
Maricopa
Tiwa
Towa Tewa
Zuni
Pecos
Yuma
Cocopah
Western Apache
Keres Tiwa
Piro
Mimbreno
Tohono O'odham
Chiricahua Apache
Apache
Mescalero Apache
Akimel O'odham
Suma
Opata
Jumano
Seri
Cahita Jova
Concho
Lipan Apache
Yaqui
Tepahue
Tarahumara
Toboso
Karankawa
Vavrohio
Mayo
Zoe
Comanito
Nio
Lagunero
Coahuiltec
Guasave
Tepehuan
Zacatec
Bocalos
Janambre
Pisones
Negrito
Tamaulipec
PACIFIC OCEAN
Gulf of California
Gulf of Mexico
Huichol
Tepecano
Colotlan
Teul
Guachichil
Guamares
Jonaz
Pame

Zuni Tribe or nation

Note: Map shown with modern boundaries.

0   300 miles

0   300 km

N

© Carl Waldman and Infobase Learning

Before Europeans arrived in the Americas, the Ancestral Puebloan were a large, diverse group of indigenous people living in the Southwest and Mexico. Subgroups like the Hopi eventually broke away and established their own tribes. This map shows the approximate location of the Hopi and other major tribes in the Southwest Culture Area just before contact with Europeans.

To begin to understand Hopi history, it is important to understand that, like many American Indian people, many Hopi feel an intimate and immediate connection with their past. Indeed, for many Hopi, time does not proceed in a straight line, as most people understand it. Rather, the past may be past and present more or less simultaneously. Anthropologists, archaeologists, and other scientists have developed a set of hypotheses about Hopi history based on evidence such as artifacts, language groupings, geology, and scientific dating methods. For traditional Hopi, these constructed histories may or may not be true, but what is important—meaningful—is the knowledge about their people that has been passed down from generation to generation since time immemorial. It is this world, this set of knowledge, in which many Hopi see themselves and their people, past, present, and future.

THE CREATION LEGEND

According to Hopi legend, when time and space began, the sun spirit (Tawa) created the First World, in which insectlike creatures lived unhappily in caves. With the goal of improvement, Tawa sent a spirit called Spider Grandmother to the world below. (Some accounts have Tawa sending his nephew, Sotuknang, to create Spider Grandmother, while still other accounts have two twins, Hard Being Woman of the West and Hard Being Woman of the East, as the creators, with Tawa merely looking on.) Spider Grandmother led the first creatures on a long trip to the Second World, during which they took on the appearance of wolves and bears. As these animals were no happier than the previous ones, however, Tawa created a new, Third World, and again sent Spider Grandmother to convey the wolves and bears there. By the time they arrived, they had become people.

Some time after the people created villages and planted corn, Spider Grandmother again appeared and taught them the skills of weaving and pottery. A hummingbird arrived bearing the fire drill, a gift from Masauwu (also written as Maasaw or Masau), a spirit from the Upper World above the sky who is the caretaker of the dead as well as the keeper of fire. Eventually, however, evil broke out among the people. Rain ceased to fall, and the corn did not grow. Perhaps with the further assistance of Spider Grandmother, or possibly with the help of bird spirits summoned through prayer, the people discovered an opening (*sipapu,* traditionally the Grand Canyon) in the sky that led to another world. More spirits caused a bamboo reed to grow up to the opening, through which the people could pass. With instructions from the priests, and with further prayer, the people with good hearts (kindness) made it to the Fourth World.

In this Fourth World, the people learned many lessons about the proper way to live. They chose their destiny, which was to live difficult lives but also in the end to outlive all other Indian tribes. They learned to worship Masauwu, who ensured that the dead return safely to the Underworld and who gave them the four sacred tablets that, in symbolic form, outlined their wanderings and their proper behavior in the Fourth World. Masauwu also told the people to watch for the *Pahána,* the Lost White Brother. Above all, the people were admonished always to remember their gods and to live in the correct way. They then split into groups, which became roughly 40 clans. Their migrations took them in all four directions, in crosses and spirals, and established their title to the land. They left records in pictographs and petroglyphs. Many legends were born from their years of wandering. When they finally reunited, members of the Bear Clan built the first village, and other clans also settled lands and brought their special ceremonies and skills.

WHAT SCIENCE SAYS

Scientists tell a different story. According to the scientific record, people have probably lived on and off in what is now Hopi territory for at least 12,000 years. For most of this time, people mainly hunted with tools called atlatls and gathered local plants to feed, clothe, and shelter themselves. Approximately 4,000 years ago, Western Pueblo people (in the areas of Acoma, Hopi, and Zuni) began to grow corn, a technology that probably came to them from the south (Mesoamerica). Scientists believe that many of the important architectural techniques, pottery-making methods, and crops of ancient Pueblo people came originally from Mesoamerica. Indeed, it is likely that the Hopi ancestors were part of the great cultural complex of aboriginal Mesoamerica—the land below, as it were.

A culture that scientists call Basketmaker became established in the Western Pueblo region roughly 1,500 to 2,000 years ago. Basketmaker people lived in caves and rock shelters, and also in small villages consisting of fewer than five pit houses that featured pole frames and brown clay mortar and, later in the period, benches and formal entryways. These people used chipped stone tools and wove baskets—some caulked with piñon pine gum—and other objects like straps, leggings, and sandals. In time, villages became larger, and the people began to make black-and-gray baked-clay pottery. By the end of the Basketmaker period, the people added beans and cotton to their crops, although most food still came from wild plants and animals. Most people continued to hunt with atlatls, although the bow and arrow was becoming more popular.

Scientists call the period from about A.D. 700 to A.D. 900 the Pueblo I period. During this time, the first villages on what are now the Hopi mesas were established. Local Indians built deeper and more elaborate pit houses and then began to abandon them in favor of dwellings completely above ground, although pit houses called *kivas* continued to be used for religious purposes. The above-ground houses were at first used only for storage. When people began to live in them, they joined the rooms to form room blocks. An increased percentage of the people's food—perhaps half—was now supplied by domesticated crops. As the people became more sedentary, they developed an increasingly complex material and artistic culture (for instance, they began to use red

The Hopi, along with other Indian groups in the region, lived in pueblo homes. Built from sandstone, many of these ancient dwellings can still be found in places throughout the Southwest, like the Grand Canyon.

and orange colors in their pottery). Scientists have found a high degree of cultural continuity between the Indians of this period and the Hopi Indians living in the area when the Spanish arrived in 1540.

Between 900 and 1250, successive Pueblo cultures (Pueblo II and III) developed. Settlements slowly grew in size, and some Western Pueblo villages featured the familiar multi-story structures built around plazas. At Hopi, home of the Hopi people, however, pit houses remained the norm longer than in other areas. Pottery developed more regional differences in the use of style and color. People developed increasingly varied and complex farming and irrigation systems, including canals, terraces, and grid systems. The town of Oraibi, still occupied today, making it the oldest continuously inhabited settlement in North America, was well established by the twelfth century.

Until the mid-thirteenth century, Hopi was characterized by hamlets, small pueblos, and isolated farmsteads. For the next 250 years or so—a period described by social scientists as Pueblo IV—the population of the Hopi mesas grew rapidly. This was due to a number of factors, including abandonment of outlying areas, presumably because of drought, as well as the encroachment of nomadic Athabaskans (Navajo and Apache), improved farming methods, and even immigration. Between 1250 and 1500, some 100 villages were scattered around the Western Pueblo region. Some were quite large, with 1,000 or more people, and almost all houses were built of sandstone and were above ground, often around plazas. The villages were linked by robust trade. Indeed, trade extended to other Western pueblos (Acoma and Zuni) as well as Eastern (Rio Grande) pueblo villages and even beyond. Population and economic growth probably led to the formation of social classes. During this period, Hopi culture became distinguished by three distinct characteristics: highly specialized farming, including selective breeding and multiple irrigation methods; artistic expression, including mural and pottery painting; and coal mining and usage.

Meanwhile, across the Atlantic Ocean, people from Western Europe developed scientific instruments and economic systems that allowed them to sail ships to distant lands. In the late fifteenth century, Christopher Columbus, sailing under a Spanish flag, encountered American Indians on the Caribbean island of Hispañola. More explorers and conquerors from Spain, and countries like England and Portugal, soon followed, and some established colonies in the New World. In 1540, the Spanish conquistador Francisco Vásquez de Coronado led an expedition into what is now New Mexico. He and his men were looking for "souls and gold," in particular, the legendary "Seven Cities of Cibola," which were rumored to be constructed of gold and other valuable minerals. They hoped to steal the gold and convert local Indians to Catholicism. They never found the gold, but they did encounter Zuni and other Indian villages, which the Spanish called *pueblos,* or towns. The Spanish explorers also visited Hopi, and their records provide the first historic accounts of life at Hopi in the early sixteenth century.

Those records reveal a population of roughly 30,000 people living in seven villages on four mesas. The Hopi at that time were primarily agriculturalists, growing corn, beans, squash, sunflowers, and cotton, although they continued ancient hunting and gathering practices as well. They had domesticated dogs and turkeys. The robust trade and contact with neighbors of earlier years had significantly diminished, as had the level and variety of agricultural practice. There was no central government. Village leadership—civil and religious—was provided by a council of elders.

Society, Politics, and Ceremony

It is important to understand that Indian societies, like societies everywhere, are dynamic over time. That is, they change—sometimes relatively quickly, sometimes relatively slowly, but they change. This is especially important to keep in mind when thinking about societies, like the Hopi, that are often described as "traditional," a word that implies that change comes very slowly, if at all. Reinforcing the notion of stasis is the very location of Hopi, located atop isolated mesas—even their physical environment seems not to change. Combined with the popular—and erroneous—notion that Indian societies didn't really change until the non-Natives interrupted their "traditional" lives, these factors make it necessary to note that any discussion of "traditional" or "precontact" Hopi life is merely a snapshot, and a fuzzy one at that, of a moment in time.

When did this moment occur? It is very difficult to say. Much evidence (oral history, art, artifacts, etc.) exists of the distant

Hopi past, but theirs was an oral culture, and for most of their history they left no written record. The Spanish, beginning in the mid-sixteenth century, were the first to describe Hopi culture in writing, but their depiction was colored by their particular perspectives. Beginning in the nineteenth century, anthropologists began to have an increasing amount of contact with the Hopi, who were still relatively isolated. Several anthropologists provided descriptions of what they considered to be "traditional" (perhaps, in their view, unchanged from time immemorial) Hopi culture. Anthropology is a social science, and although we tend to think of "science" as somehow "real" and "true," it turns out that anthropologists have their own biases, and one anthropologist may describe things quite differently from another.

To talk about "traditional" Hopi culture, then, is at best a gross simplification and at worst completely misleading. And yet, we must make a try! For the purposes of this book, specific dates or periods will be referred to whenever possible. Generalizations unaccompanied by a date reference will roughly refer to the late nineteenth century, since that time followed a long period of relative isolation, is relatively heavily documented, and preceded the major changes of the twentieth century.

SOCIAL ORGANIZATION

According to the *Handbook of North American Indians, Vol. 9 Southwest,* the Hopi had over time evolved a social structure consisting of "small household units, held together in strong obligatory kin groups within the manageable bounds of cooperative work groups." This social structure allowed the Hopi to survive in a setting that was marginal to human existence. Early Spanish accounts of the Hopi report that they lived in seven small villages on four mesas. By about 1900, "the Hopi continued to live in some six, permanent compact communities ranging in size from about 160 to 880 persons," write Scott Rushforth and Steadman Upham in *A Hopi Social History.* Each community was independent from

The complex society of the Hopi includes kivas, underground rooms built for religious groups. Clans own their own kivas, but members of other clans can join and participate in a kiva group.

the others and consisted of several organizational levels both vertical (hierarchical) and horizontal (non-hierarchical). The household existed at the most basic level. Households consisted of several generations of biologically related women and their husbands if they were married. When a couple married, they lived with the wife's female relatives. Indeed, women related through their mothers' line owned the houses in which they lived.

At the next level of complexity, Hopi society recognized lineages formed by descent from female relatives. Lineage members consisted of people within a single household and different households who traced their descent to the same woman. These lineages in turn came together to form clans, the next most inclusive organizational level in Hopi society.

Clans, the heart of Hopi society, were (and are) similar to lineages, but they traced their descent to an unknown, perhaps even mythic, woman, and as such could include a greater number of female descent groups than those that could prove descent from a known ancestor. These clans had specific names derived from mythological events. Perhaps their most defining characteristic was that they conferred ownership of any number of valued commodities, including farms and ceremonies, along with items associated with those ceremonies. Each clan also owned a house, which served as a clan meeting place and as the repository of its most important possessions. The principal clans—the ones who originally entered Hopi from the four directions—are Bear, Parrot, Eagle, and Badger.

More inclusive and complex (although less culturally important) than clans were social organizations called phratries, or groups of clans that recognized a connection with one another. Unlike clans, phratries were not named, but like them their connections involved mythological events. Although members of the same phratry might or might not be related by blood, they viewed their relationship as similar to kinship.

POLITICAL ORGANIZATION

According to archaeological evidence, ancient Hopi societies were relatively egalitarian and politically decentralized. In the late nineteenth century, Hopi villages remained, or had again become, highly independent. The Hopi "tribe" did not exist. Neither, for that matter, did political leadership as we know it. For all intents and purposes, politics and religion were inseparable. The priests— clan-based leaders of the religious societies—provided leadership, and the priest of the most important society served as the first among equals: the village leader, or *kikmongwi*. This person, traditionally a member of the Bear Clan, exercised authority that was more moral than political. He and the other priests promoted civic virtue and proper behavior. The village leader's counterpart in enforcement and external matters was the *qaletaqmongwi*, or war leader. The relative authority of these leaders varied according to the peacefulness of the times.

RELIGIOUS ORGANIZATION AND CEREMONIALISM

Standing in harmony with the complex system of vertical social relationships in Hopi society around the dawn of the twentieth century was a traditional system of horizontal religious or ceremonial relationships. In keeping with their relatively independent character, Hopi communities created individual religious cycles as well as cycles observed by all of the villages. (The following discussion omits the complexities of individual village ceremonial cycles.) The Hopi also created a number of religious societies that were voluntary in nature. These organizations were linked to the people's religious ceremonies in very specific ways. That is, each group accepted the responsibility "for the performance of a specific religious ceremony at a definite time of year and in a particular kiva," according to *A Hopi Social History*. Religious societies included the *katsina* society as well as separate men's and women's societies.

Hopi religious societies were linked to, although distinct from, clans. As noted above, clans owned paraphernalia associated with specific ceremonies performed by a particular religious society. In fact, they could own the ceremonies themselves, and part of the rights and privileges of ownership included providing the priests, or leaders, of a society's religious ceremonies. It is important to note, however, that only the leaders were associated with a specific clan—most of the people who were members of a religious society belonged to many clans. The same was true of kiva groups. Kivas are underground chambers—symbolizing the underground place of emergence—that serve as the sites of religious activity. The kivas and their associated ceremonies were owned by particular clans (although not necessarily the same clans), but membership in kiva groups cut across many clans. In this way, the Hopi organized their society in a complex and interwoven system that maximized political autonomy, religious cohesiveness, and social connectedness.

Hopi religious belief is founded on the premise that the people, guided through many years of wanderings to unite in a homeland at what they considered to be the center of the universe, were divinely charged with maintaining the "universal pattern of Creation . . . in every act of . . . daily life" according to Frank Waters's *Book of the Hopi*. How to remain faithful to this plan? The Hopi recognize, as do many of the world's people, the undying soul, or life force. The Hopi people believe that the people rose to live on Earth from an underground place. In death, according to Hopi belief, the spirit descends to reinhabit that underground world, a place very similar to the world above.

The two worlds—above and below, spiritual and temporal—exist in a certain dualistic harmony with each other, a happy situation made possible by acknowledging that relationship and keeping it in balance through complex space-time-number-color interrelationships, combined with activities such as singing, dancing, and smoking (wild tobacco, which was significantly different from the modern packaged variety) that form the core of Hopi ceremonialism.

Reflecting the close association between the world of the living and that of the dead, spirits play an integral role in the land of the living. They are associated with clouds and with benevolent supernatural entities called *katsinam* (the plural of katsina), which inhabit the San Francisco Peaks just north of Flagstaff, Arizona. Katsinam, however, are not just spirits of the dead. They are, Susanne and Jake Page write, "the spirits of all things in the universe, of rocks, stars, animals, plants, and ancestors who have lived good lives." At least 300 katsinam exist. Some are no longer current, and new ones have been created. Each has different meanings

The Hopi honor the katsinam, the "spirits of all things in the universe." Male dancers who perform in annual ceremonies as katsinam wear elaborate masks and costumes to represent these revered spirits. Dolls like this are meant to teach children to recognize katsinam.

and representations. Children learn the names and purposes of the different katsinam through wooden dolls. Katsinam are, on the whole, benevolent, but, as mentioned earlier, the benefits that spirits bestow (like controlling the weather) require certain reciprocal behaviors and obligations in the form of prayer and ceremonialism, and in day-to-day life. This is why many katsina ceremonies feature mutual gift giving and why katsinam themselves are said to inspire, or demand, good behavior—in effect, they exist to ensure that the Hopi live in the balanced or "correct" way.

Not surprisingly, katsinam figured—and continue to figure—prominently in Hopi ceremonialism. During the first half of the calendar year (the timing of Hopi ceremonies is determined by solar or lunar observation), the ceremonies were marked by masked dancers impersonating the katsinam. (Although katsinam could be either male or female, the dancers were all men.) *Powamu* is the season's first full katsina ceremony. Occurring in February and associated with bean planting, it heralds the new growing season and asks the katsinam to help ensure a bountiful harvest. Powamu is also associated with coming of age, for this is the time for initiation into the Powamu and katsina societies. Those 10- and 11-year-olds who will be joining the society receive religious instruction in the kiva. Following the instruction, the katsinam themselves enter the kiva and the night-time ceremony begins in earnest, complete with dancing and drumming.

As spring progresses, so does the prominence of katsinam—in dances, and also as reminders of social convention, especially for children. The dances, which also feature the appearance of clowns, are closely related to planting. The clowns play an important role—embodying wrong social behavior, they are soon put in their place by the katsinam for all to see. The presence of clowns in the morality play makes people more receptive to the messages of proper social convention and encourages a crucial human trait: a keen sense of humor. The final katsina ceremony takes place in July, when the last crops have been planted and the harvest

Katsinam in the Twenty-first Century

Katsinam have been part of Hopi religion and ceremonialism since the fourteenth century and possibly long before that. Franciscan missionaries arrived about 1630 and probably had some influence on Hopi culture. Their expulsion in the 1680 Pueblo Revolt brought an end to Catholic influence and attacks on ceremonies, but Pueblo refugees from that conflict who resettled at Hopi brought their own cultural traditions, which doubtless influenced Hopi ceremonialism. During the next 200 years, only sporadic cultural influences from the outside (Native and non-Native) influenced Hopi cultural and religious practice. Significant contact with the Americans began in the late nineteenth century, including the establishment of schools and the arrival of various government officials, scientists, and missionaries.

In response to their demands, some Hopi began to provide non-Natives with ceremonial objects, including katsinam (some of which were made to order). Moreover, Hopi carvers responded to the demand for katsina "dolls," or *tihü,* by greatly increasing their production. In the twentieth century, historical events like World War II and postwar affluence and mobility produced profound cultural changes at Hopi, as elsewhere. Not surprisingly, this increased cultural contact (combined with environmental changes caused by factors like overgrazing and game scarcity) altered the katsina ceremonies in various

begins to come in. Known as *Niman,* or "to go home," it marks the departure of the katsinam back to their home in the San Francisco Peaks. (Since everything is reversed in the spirit world, the katsinam are needed for the winter solstice there.) This deeply spiritual ceremony encourages people to contemplate the messages of the ways. New materials, such as saddle leather, felt, and commercial cloths and yarns, crept into the manufacture of masks. Pre-dyed feathers might be bought in department stores (especially after the passage of the Endangered Species Act of 1973 curtailed the use of certain bird feathers). Cattle parts replaced those formerly obtained from buffalo. In the non-material sphere, under pressure from various non-Hopi "moralists," some katsinam that were overtly sexual, in connection with rituals concerning germination and fertility, have been altered to minimize, or in some cases eliminate, their sexuality. Generational conflicts have interfered with the essential transmission of complex religious and ceremonial knowledge.

Today, katsina "dolls" have become staples in gift shops across the Southwest. The relatively few katsina "dolls" made by Hopi carvers are subtly altered so that their religious meaning is erased. (More conservative Hopi object to any commercialism of their religious objects, however altered.) Katsinam made by some Hopi master carvers command considerable value as works of art. At the same time, many are made by non-Hopi who do not know the traditional designs. In some cases, mass-produced imitation "katsinam" are available for sale. Certainly among non-Hopi, but even in some Hopi homes, katsina dolls are primarily used for decoration. Nevertheless, and despite all the changes, Hopi society remains strong, and katsina ceremonies, among others, continue to infuse the Hopi spirit with meaning, balance, and a connectedness to the ancient past.

katsinam and their own behavior, so that the rain will come and the harvest will be good.

Following the season of the katsina dances come non-katsina ceremonials, such as the snake-antelope ceremony and the flute ceremony. The former, which does in fact feature men handling snakes, including rattlesnakes, and placing them in their mouths, is essentially a rain dance, snakes being messengers of the underworld. The latter, which is also meant to encourage rainfall, re-enacts the emergence into the Fourth World. As the harvest begins to come in, a series of women's dances, celebrating the power of curing and regeneration, concludes the annual ceremonial cycle. In November, *Wuwutsim,* a ritual of the four men's societies, heralds the start of the ceremonial cycle and, in some years, includes a male initiation ceremony. *Soyal,* perhaps the most important ceremony of all, marks the winter solstice. The katsinam begin to return to the villages during Soyal, which acknowledges their glad tidings from the sun and marks the cycle of renewal.

Several common elements characterize Hopi ceremonials. The Crier Chief announces ceremonies from the roof of a house. *Páhos,* or prayer feathers, are usually made from eagle feathers. According to legend, the eagle offered himself as a messenger to the Sun/Creator above. There are many kinds of prayer feathers, but whatever the kind of páho, its manufacture is accompanied by spiritual intentionality and tobacco smoke offerings. Cornmeal is essential to Hopi ceremonialism, corn being the staff of life for the Hopi and for many agricultural Indian groups. It is used in a variety of ways, depending on the particular ceremony. In addition to dancing, foot races accompany many Hopi ceremonies. Major ceremonies, which traditionally lasted for eight (or 16) days and nights, are followed by several days of ritual purification in the kiva before normal life may be resumed.

After automobile transportation made Hopi more accessible to outsiders, some ceremonies began to attract crowds, due primarily to their colorful and dramatic nature. The Hopi are happy to share some of their culture with outsiders. In recent years, however, they have closed some of their ceremonies, or parts of ceremonies, to public viewing to protect the ancient knowledge and the sacredness of the occasion.

Related to, but distinct from, the religious ceremonies are a series of social dances. While not specifically religious, social dances do involve significant preparation in the kiva. The two-day Buffalo Dance is an example of a social dance. Held in January, in one or two villages, this dance harks back to the days when the people hunted buffalo, or bison. The Butterfly Dance, held in late summer, is another social dance. The Hopi also once held an annual war ceremony in the fall, but it is no longer practiced. The next chapter will discuss Hopi material culture, some of which figures in both religious ceremonies and social dances.

Material Culture

Ancient projectile points constitute the archaeological evidence of human habitation in the Black Mesa region before 10,000 B.C. The paleo-Indian population of the area was probably small and mobile. Local traditions were difficult to distinguish before about 3000 B.C. Beginning with the period that archaeologists call Basketmaker II (roughly 100 B.C. to A.D. 400), sites near Hopi (but not at Hopi) yield quantities of baskets (hence the name of the archaeological period) and other artifacts of plant material as well as chipped stone tools. Other artifacts characteristic of Basketmaker II sites in the region include wooden gaming dice, shell beads, and wooden tools and household items (such as combs).

Most tools, such as metates and manos (grinding tools typically used to process whole grains, like corn, into meal), as well as axes and knives, were made of stone. *Piiki* stones (a variety of which is still used at Hopi) were a kind of griddle, used to make *piiki* (a very thin wafer) out of corn gruel. Most stone tools were made of local chert (a silica-rich sedimentary rock), petrified wood, obsidian, jasper, basalt, or quartzite. Perhaps around A.D. 1100, as methods of agriculture began to diversify, the people began to use farm implements such as hoes, typically made from sandstone. Other stone tools of that period included grinding stones (multipurpose grinders) and items used to flake other stone tools (to create sharp edges or finger grips) or to shape tools made from wood, like the atlatl and the bow and arrow. People also chipped stone for use as projectile points, knives, scrapers, and other such tools. Sometimes these tools were also acquired through trade.

Moreover, besides stone, people used shell and wood by around 1300. The people obtained most shells locally—from the Little Colorado River—as well as in trade from as far away as the Gulf of California and the Gulf of Mexico. Shells were often worked, usually by grinding, carving, or drilling, and were used for both tools and ornaments (such as beads and bracelets).

Wood was not abundant at Hopi, but some tools were, and are, made from wood, primarily from the cottonwood tree, although oak and juniper were used as well. Wooden planting sticks might have either a stone or (later) an iron blade. Wood eventually supplanted stone as the raw material for hoes. Hand trowels were also made of wood, as were some boxes and cups, dolls, drums, and parts of masks. Rakes used to clean brush from the fields consisted of a peeled, three-tined branch of a juniper tree, with the tines secured by a lashed wooden rod. The people picked prickly-pear fruit with the help of wooden tweezers. The wooden fire drill was in use until early in the twentieth century. Baby cradles were made mainly of wood, with soft, shredded cedar bark generally providing diaper material. Weaving tools, including upright looms, were generally made of wood as well.

Local animals also provided material for manufactured goods such as clothing and tools. Despite its harsh environment, Hopi was home to many animals, including fish, reptiles, lizards, birds,

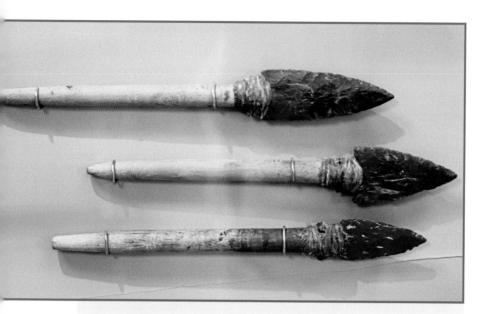

Hopi weapons and tools were handmade from available materials. Because trees are scarce in the Southwest, the Hopi mainly used different types of stone, such as basalt and obsidian.

and mammals such as rodents, rabbits, deer, and antelope. The people traditionally worked bone to make a great variety of tools and ornaments, including awls, hairpins, tubes, rings, musical instruments, and beads, and other parts of an animal, such as the horn, were also used. Larger animals were driven into corrals or, after the sixteenth century, hunted with the bow and arrow on horseback. Smaller animals and birds might be caught in a variety of nets, snares, and deadfalls or killed with a distinctive oak boomerang, which allowed for capture or killing without mutilation or the shedding of blood. Hunting was typically an activity associated with religious practice. By about 1900 the burro (a sixteenth-century Spanish import), which is adept at surviving in harsh environments, had become indispensible to the Hopi.

Hopi people were making baskets and pots at least as early as A.D. 500. Woven mats, similar to some basketry technology, were employed to wrap the dead, among other uses. Hopi women made carrying baskets and some cradles of wicker. Most baskets were of the coiled variety—typically a bundle of grass stems was coiled and sewn together with strips of yucca leaf and worked with an awl of bone (deer or, more recently sheep). Baskets were often decorated with symbols of birds, or parts of birds, in combination with clouds, rainbows, and sometimes stars.

Hopi women were, and are, expert potters. Around A.D. 500, most pottery was of a gray or black-on-gray color, but within several hundred years, the people began to include colors like red, yellow, and orange, applied with yucca-leaf brushes. Knowledge of pottery making may have come from the south (Mexico) as early as 2500 B.C. Among the pottery items in use around 1900 were salt containers, bowls, jars, vases, and spoons. Gourds, too, provided the Hopi with a number of items, including dippers, spoons, cups, bottles, and parts of masks, as well as a variety of musical instruments, like horns, trumpets, rattles (which might also be made from shells and dried berries), flutes, and bells.

HOUSING

Hopi people lived in various types of dwellings toward the end of the first millennium and into the beginning of the second. Beginning in the period known as Basketmaker III (A.D. 400–700), pit houses, of varying depth and size, were most common. Later pit houses were rectangular, perhaps 10 feet (3 meters) to a side and 1 to 2 feet deep (.3 to .6 meters deep). Houses made of sandstone and clay mortar were built on top of the ground. There were separate rooms for living and storage as well as round, subterranean kivas. During the Pueblo I period, the people began to abandon pit houses in favor of the above-ground style. These were also made of sandstone plastered with adobe mortar and typically contained several rooms and a hearth.

By the time of the Spanish contact, some of these structures were quite large, with hundreds of rooms. Many of the large houses were built around plazas, and villages also featured square

Housing structures evolved from a pit in the ground to tall structures with underground kivas. As Hopi villages grew larger, the pueblo houses were built higher and people climbed ladders to enter their homes.

or circular kivas. Distinctive one- or two-story pueblo housing featured sandstone and adobe walls and roof beams of pine and juniper. The people entered their dwellings via ladders that extended through openings in the roof.

ENERGY

Coal mining and use, at least as early as the thirteenth century, constituted one of the defining aspects of Hopi society. The Hopi may have been the only Native American group to use coal during this period. Coal was plentiful in Hopi country, as it is today, and similar to today the people used it for heating and cooking. They also set paving stones in beds of coal ash, and they used the ash, when still hot, to fire their pottery.

Hopi people used two techniques to mine coal. One consisted of using stone picks and hammers as well as potsherds (pottery fragments), scraping the earth to reveal the coal below. The other was underground mining. During the period in question, the Hopi probably mined roughly 450 pounds (200 kilograms) of coal daily at the deposits near the village of Awatovi. Considering the technology as well as the population, it is likely that coal mining was a major activity during this period and that, at least until the seventeenth century, coal was the dominant source of fuel at Hopi.

In the early seventeenth century, the use of coal declined in favor of wood and, as a means for firing pottery, sheep dung. According to archaeologist J.O. Brew, the reasons for this are unclear but may have included depletion of readily accessible supplies as well as new technology (such as iron tools, carts, and donkeys to pull the carts) introduced by the Spanish, which made gathering wood and shoveling dung a great deal easier.

DRESS

Men sometimes wore tanned deerskin shirt-coats and leggings, when deer and antelope were abundant or, more commonly, when these items were obtained in trade (the Hopi traded finished woven products to the Havasupai and Apache people in exchange for items such as meat, hides, piñon nuts, and shells). In the colder winter months, people supplemented these clothes with buckskin and buffalo hides. Moccasins, worn by men and women, were also made of leather, although these may reflect the influence of other groups—Plains people and/or Navajo or Apache—and were likely preceded by the use of sandals.

Generally, though, the Hopi style of dress was more influenced by their neighbors to the south than to the east, and weaving, performed by men, was the predominant technology related to clothing. The traditional fabric materials were native cotton and

Weaving

Weaving is an ancient art among the Hopi people. Long before the arrival of non-Natives, Hopi men grew short-staple cotton, which they spun into thread and sewed into fabric. The Spanish, who arrived in the mid-sixteenth century, introduced sheep to the Hopi, and Hopi weavers soon became known for their fine wool as well as cotton goods. Until the twentieth century, all dyes were natural and plant based, such as cochineal or carmine dye (taken from insects that feed on prickly-pear cactus) and indigo. Hopi men used an upright loom to weave a number of items, including blankets, belts, kilts, and sashes. Woven items, especially of a sacred nature, were often decorated with embroidery and tassels. Colors (such as black, green, red, and yellow) and designs (birds, clouds) were not merely decorative but typically had religious meaning.

shredded yucca fiber. Whipping the seeds on sand with a bundle of rods was the method of separating the cotton from the seed. Woven material was often dyed with indigo, which was introduced by the Spanish.

In the sixteenth century, men likely wore cotton sarongs, finished on the edges, wrapped around the waist, and held in place by a woven belt. By about 1900, men often wore ponchos with short sleeves of dark blue or black woolen cloth. Men also wore shell and stone bead necklaces—these were generally acquired in trade from other Pueblo groups. Both men and women also wore rabbit-skin robes, the fur being cut into strips, wound around a cord, and twined together with wool, cotton, or hair. Before the sixteenth century these robes were often overlaid with, or made

The Hopi have a long tradition of weaving and dyeing cloth, and various sewn garments and hairstyles marked important events or social status. Young unmarried women, for instance, wore a long, brown and blue blanket, with one shoulder revealed, and fashioned their hair into the shape of squash blossoms.

from, turkey feathers. Ceremonial kilts as well as sashes were made of woven cotton variously decorated. By 1900 or so, sheep and goats provided much of the raw material for clothing and blankets.

Married women generally wore woven dark brown and woven blue garments, essentially blankets sewn together with an opening for the right arm while the left arm and shoulder were free. These might be embroidered with colorful yarns. Depending on the weather, and particularly in ceremonies, they might also wear woven shoulder blankets, or shawls. Unmarried women generally wore the same outfit except that they also wore wood and turquoise earrings. In the late nineteenth century, unmarried women also wore their hair in the shape of squash blossoms. A special white blanket, very finely woven and embroidered, was part of a woman's marriage outfit.

Farming and Diet

The Hopi are well known as an agricultural people. Roughly 5,000 years ago, people ancestral to today's Hopi lived in hunter-gatherer bands that moved to take advantage of changing natural resources. Their food consisted of various plants (including piñon nuts, seeds, roots, berries, grasses) and animals (birds as well as large and small game). It is likely that these small bands were able to procure sufficient food to maintain stability. However, the Hopi began to grow corn as early as roughly 2000 B.C., or shortly after cultigens first appeared north of Mexico. They started to grow corn even though rainfall in their area (roughly 5,000 feet, or 1,524 meters, in elevation) seldom exceeds 10 inches (25 centimeters) per year, mainly in the form of summer downpours, droughts are not uncommon, winds are frequently strong, and frosts limit the growing season to roughly four months. Why did the people introduce corn (maize) and other crops, such as squash, into their diets when they presumably had had enough to eat and water resources were so uncertain?

Scientists put forth two answers to this question. One, with a more or less stable food supply, the population grew slowly, and at some point it began to outstrip the available food supply. Without the option of agriculture, the population would have simply adjusted itself to the natural food supply. In this case, though, the need for innovation sparked by population pressures found an outlet in the latest technology—cultivation—which provided an opportunity to supplement wild food and thus increase population to some degree. The other answer is that they didn't—or at least, they did, but only very slowly. In the beginning, some bands probably planted a bit of corn in favorable locations, tending their crops when they could but maintaining their rounds of hunting and gathering. The shift toward agriculture took place over thousands of years, as the people created new farming technologies and learned to take advantage of the microclimates that existed in the area. Cultivated crops probably did not constitute the main food source until roughly A.D. 1000, and even then they never wholly supplanted hunting and gathering.

What were these plants that the ancestral Hopi grew? The most basic was corn, or maize, which is likely descended from a Mexican wild grass. Indians living in present-day Mexico were cultivating maize and other crops, like squash, beans, gourds, chili peppers, avocado, and amaranth, by roughly 3500 B.C. Over the years, people developed hardier and larger varieties of maize. They also introduced new crops, such as kidney beans (roughly 2,000 years after the introduction of maize). Beans and corn eaten together provide what is known as a complete protein, which contains an adequate proportion of all of the essential amino acids required for a healthy human diet. Ancestral Hopis probably began to cultivate squash around 1 B.C., although its first appearance in the American Southwest probably coincides with that of maize. Sunflowers were a late adoption. Cotton, grown for its oil-rich seeds

Corn is a staple food in the Americas, and the Hopi grew several varieties of the crop. Corn can be ground into flour and used to bake bread or other dishes.

as well as the fiber, has been present for at least 2,500 years. After contact with non-Natives, the Hopi experimented with various non-Native crops and quickly learned that peaches and apricots would be successful for the same reasons as the native crops they had adapted, including their long, deep roots.

IRRIGATION AND INNOVATIONS

Eventually, the Hopi developed a tremendous amount of skill in producing relatively high-yield crops. Farming innovations, including selective breeding of plants and breakthroughs in irrigation, as well as planting different varieties of crops in appropriate microclimates (elevation, soil type, wind, slope, drainage), are the single most important explanation for the ability of the Hopi to

Corn

Corn is as central to the Hopi people (and to many other Indian groups of the Americas) as are air and water. Despite living in an environment with poor soil and scant rain, the Hopi for centuries have made maize their main food staple. Its existence harks back to their creation story, in which Hopi ancestors, upon arriving in this world, were offered several varieties of corn in which their destiny would be reflected. They chose the short blue ear, indicating that their lives would be difficult but that they would outlive all the other peoples on Earth.

The Hopi also regard maize as sacred because it embodies both male and female elements. Like mother's milk, it nourishes the people who spring from, and depend on, their mother (Earth). The rounded ear of corn is considered female, while the straight tassel is considered male. A perfect ear of corn that is used ritually is called the Corn Mother.

Cornmeal is an essential part of Hopi ceremonial practice. It is used to make paths for katsinam, to block trails during the Wuwutsim ceremony, to welcome katsina dancers, to greet the rising sun, as part of new baby ceremonies, and in many other ways.

thrive in their harsh, dry environment. If one or more crops failed (because of climatic factors and/or insect or animal depredations), others elsewhere would succeed. Of course, the Hopi also chose their settlement location carefully. The mesas are drained by streams that carry silt and sand toward the plateau below. There, prevailing southwest winds blow the sand back up to form dunes, which in turn tend to trap water. Thus the precise location of Hopi lands, combined with wind and rain patterns and the sandy soil, has meant that the area is favored with more water retention following rain, and a greater number of permanent springs, than nearby lands. This being the case, the soil is less likely to dry out and crops are not as likely to fail from lack of water.

Moreover, the Hopi learned that, to take advantage of the conditions in their part of the world, they needed to grow crops with deep roots, such as beans and maize. Indeed, over time the Hopi adapted these crops to grow roots even longer and deeper than the varieties they had initially grown. Hopi people also learned to plant breaks (using basketry or brush held in place by large stones) to guard their crops against winds that might ordinarily blow too much sand in their direction and, by roughly A.D. 1000, they had developed various water control devices as well.

Besides farming crops with deep roots in protected areas, the Hopi practiced (and continue to practice) distinct types of "dry" (non-irrigated) farming. One type involved planting in floodplains that received water when streams overflowed their banks during storms. Overflows were controlled to a certain degree by the use of check dams, or dams placed across small channels to slow water flow and control erosion. Another type, known as ak-chin agriculture, involved planting by the mouth of an arroyo (wash), so that, following a heavy rain, water flowed through the arroyo and onto the fields.

In the past, farming tools consisted of a very small number of items, such as the wooden digging stick and dibble. Hoes were made of stone, then wood. Later, the people adopted the horse and plow, and still later, mechanized farm equipment. Crops were transported using baskets until the people switched to burros (carrying blankets filled with corn, and then pulling wagons) and, later, to trucks.

The gradual adoption of agriculture also led, not surprisingly, to other material changes. Large, secure storage pits, for instance, made it possible to retain agricultural foodstuff for months or even years, which significantly helped the people to guard against

In order for the Hopi to grow crops successfully in the harsh climate of the Southwest, they had to develop better agricultural methods and tools. Advanced irrigation systems, plant diversity, and the plow helped the Hopi to yield more crops. In turn, their population grew with the abundance of food.

hunger. Unlike baskets, pottery, while taken up later than farming, offered a way to keep perishables away from insects and small animals. Corn was typically baked in pits and then stored for future use. Beans were usually dried and stored for later preparation by soaking and boiling. Squash was cultivated mainly for the seeds, which provide substantially more calories, minerals, and vitamins than the flesh. Seeds were eaten dried, while the flesh of the squash was generally either boiled and eaten fresh or dried in strips.

By the end of the first millennium, the people had developed a sustainable agricultural society. Closely related to that stability, the accompanying dependence on rain and other climatic conditions, and the existence of food surpluses were cultural developments often associated with agricultural people, such as villages, sophisticated religious practice, complex social organization, and a rich artistic tradition. When the Spanish arrived in the mid-sixteenth century, they found Hopi agricultural practice developed to the point that we now consider "traditional."

FARMING TODAY

Today, autonomous villages are still associated with specific lands. Fields, located below the mesa tops in the washes and small valleys that separate the plateaus, are divided into small sections (usually less than 10 acres) and assigned to clans. Sections are typically owned or controlled by the women but planted by the men. Direct contact with traditional crops is still carried out by hand, although some Hopi use tractors for planting and plowing. Pest control (against worms and coyotes) and fertilizing is also done by hand, in keeping with centuries-old tradition. The people continue to control erosion of traditional fields through windbreaks and check dams. Some women and girls still learn how to store crops and seeds to avoid mold and mildew, although storage containers aren't always "home made" and may include items such as galvanized trash cans. Perhaps most importantly, farming of traditional crops, especially corn, is still the center of Hopi spirituality. The people remember their history and the covenant with their guardian spirits, and they continue to perform their agricultural and ceremonial cycle with a prayerful heart.

The Hopi grow roughly 25 varieties of corn, as well as varieties of beans, squash, melons, gourds, sunflowers, chili peppers, peaches, apricots, onions, and other vegetables. Besides traditional fields, some people now grow newer crops in irrigated gardens. They also continue to hunt and to make use of numerous wild plants. Lamb and beef have taken their place in the Hopi diet, as has store-bought food.

Besides the technological changes that have accompanied some aspects of modern farming at Hopi, the people face non-technological challenges that have been less easy to adapt to. The United States government does not recognize Hopi "ownership" of their ancestral land. One result of this situation is that Hopis have difficulty securing loans (not having title, they cannot use the land as collateral) and thus financing agricultural improvements. Another obstacle to securing loans is the people's relatively low income, their difficulty negotiating the complex world of American finance, and the use of their crops almost exclusively for subsistence (that is, they have no commercial value). There are ways around these obstacles, but they are not easy, and some are not even possible without changes in federal law and policy.

Artistic Traditions

Artists of all cultures are drawn to their work by a number of factors, not the least of which is sheer talent and creativity. Among the Hopi, art, especially the traditional arts of pottery and weaving, is also a manifestation of a spiritual connection with the earth. Through their work, Hopi artists use the bounty of the earth to express their inner creativity and to nourish the lives of their people, in both utilitarian and ceremonial ways.

In roughly the fourteenth century, the Hopi people experienced many changes. Their villages expanded and consolidated, and their entire worldview may have shifted as the clan migrations came to an end and Hopi ceremonialism assumed its classic outline. Artistically, too, ancient symmetrical, geometric, repetitive forms began to give way to asymmetrical, abstract, curvilinear designs, along with realistic portrayals of life forms.

For many Hopi artists of the past generation or two, creative inspiration came with the "Red Power" movement of the 1960s and 1970s, part of the general ethnic reawakening of America at the time. Many young Hopi men and women who had absorbed negative images about their own people rediscovered the value and beauty of their heritage. Some who had left the reservation moved back and became acquainted, or reacquainted, with their traditions, artistic and otherwise.

Today, as in days of old, each mesa, and, to some extent, each village enjoys a degree of cultural specialization. So it is with the arts. Another theme that pervades Hopi art is the extent to which Hopi culture and, indeed, the Hopi people themselves, have been exploited in the service of both tourism and a type of "Southwest" and generic "Indian" mysticism. We must also note that the Hopi are engaged in other arts, including photography and poetry, in addition to the ones profiled here.

BASKETRY

Like their forebears, today's Hopi basket weavers make three kinds of baskets, and the type is identified by location: plaited (braided) on First Mesa, coiled on Second Mesa, and wicker on Third Mesa. Of the three, plaiting is the oldest technique, although today basket making is most active on Second and Third Mesas. Plaiting uses material from the same plant, while coiling and wicker use material from different plants. Basket weavers came, and to a large extent still come, from members of two of the three women's societies, Lalkont and O'waqolt.

Baskets had, and have, many uses, both utilitarian (sifter baskets, trays, baby cradles, burden baskets) and ceremonial (plaques, although even these are now made for commercial purposes). Very early baskets were even used for cooking (hot stones were placed in baskets and dropped into water to make it boil), although this function was eventually taken over by pottery. Baskets were, and are, intimately bound up in the people's social interactions. Plaques (flat baskets) were traditionally used almost exclusively for rituals (including rites of passage and basket dances). Hopis

Basket weaving is an important traditional art in Hopi culture, as the baskets are used in everyday activities as well as important ceremonies. Baskets can be woven into several different styles. *Above,* three unmarried Hopi women weave coiled baskets.

started to make them for commercial sale in the middle of the twentieth century, although plaques are still used ceremonially and for "paybacks" (for work or favors) and gifts.

Ancient coiled baskets have a foundation (warp) of peeled rods covered with split-leaf material. Today, women make coiled baskets, decorated with colorful designs, from galleta grass stems, and for the weave (weft) they use yucca leaves. Indeed, yucca is the most important element of coiled baskets. Colors are all natural and come from the plant at different stages of development;

weavers intimately familiar with the yucca know exactly when to harvest it, and what to do with it when harvested, to produce the colors they seek. Once harvested, yucca leaves need to be carefully cleaned, split, and dried. Plants used in dyeing, such as Navajo tea (*siita*) and Hopi tea (*hohoisi*), must also be carefully gathered and prepared. Black dye traditionally came from sunflowers, although today most women use commercial product.

Sifter baskets are traditionally of the plaited variety. Materials for the central ring have largely transitioned away from traditional sumac to other plants and even metal, after which yucca is typically used to complete the piece. Plaited baskets are generally less tight, and more flexible, than other types of baskets.

The wicker technique is several hundred years old, but its origins are largely unknown—it may have come from clans migrating from the south. Ancestral Hopi did use a wicker weaving technique, but not for making baskets—they used it to make yucca-leaf sandals. One of the earliest wicker baskets found near Hopi was a plaque dating to the fourteenth century that was made using a very similar technique to today's Third Mesa plaques. The process of making today's wicker baskets, from material collecting, to preparing, to weaving, is very complex. It requires a great deal of hard work but also provides great potential for artistic creativity.

POTTERY

The Hopi people have been making pottery for roughly 1,500 years. The earliest pottery was white, black, and red. When the Spanish arrived at Hopi in 1540, they found the people producing distinctive yellow-ware pottery in large quantities and trading it throughout the Southwest. By 1400 or so, Hopi women were making pottery now known as Sikyatki Polychrome.

Ceramic traditions are especially developed on First Mesa. Like basketry, pottery is a woman's craft. Traditional Hopi potters do not use a potter's wheel. As practiced around 1900, clay was dug from sources on and near the mesa. Potters kneaded it on flat stones

Passed down from one generation to the next, crafting pottery is a traditional activity for Hopi women. Nampeyo (*above*), a famous Hopi pottery artist, was the first to revive the ancient style of Hopi pottery and created beautiful, low pots with wide shoulders.

to smooth it and remove impurities. Ground sandstone might be added to the clay as a temper, or hardener. Pots were either molded or coiled, with gourds or perhaps squash rinds used to smooth the developing pot. After drying, the potter polished the piece with a smooth stone. Paints were all natural at this time, either mineral or plant based. They were applied in the traditional way, with a yucca leaf. Once dried again, the pots were fired in sheep's dung.

Hopi pottery went into a long, slow decline after the arrival of the Spanish. But beginning around 1880, Hopi women began to pattern their pottery on ancient designs, such as low, wide-shouldered jars and bowls painted with stylized birds, butterflies, and animals, due in part to the attention of archaeologists and art collectors. Nampeyo, a superb artist and craftswoman, was the most famous of these "Hopi Revival" potters. Inspired by the old forms and designs, they turned craft into art and ushered in a whole new era of Hopi pottery.

Of course, Hopi women are, typically, extremely busy. As part of a tightly knit society with a strong clan system, Hopi women spend a good deal of their lives doing work associated with food. During harvest, women winnow and store beans; burn the dried stalks to get ashes for making *piiki;* husk, dry, and stack corn; and other such tasks. Men harvest the crops, but it is up to women to process the foodstuffs and store them for winter. They must also gather any number of wild foods. There are many occasions that require them to provide food to their immediate as well as their extended family. Stews, *piiki,* tamales, and breads are just some of the foods that they prepare. Basket makers and potters must find time for this work in their "spare" time. Often it is older women, whose children are grown, who have more time for making baskets and pots, although by then many women suffer a loss of vision that makes creative work more difficult.

TEXTILE WEAVING

At least 1,400 years ago, people living in present-day Hopi were weaving belts of native fiber, such as yucca. Hopi men have been weaving cotton for almost as long, and they began to use wool when the Spanish brought sheep in the sixteenth century. Most early items were made in simple weave, but some were in twills, tapestry, and other more complex weaves, and were decorated with brocade and embroidery. The most common color was black, followed by red and brown.

When cotton batting became available in local trading posts in the late nineteenth century, Hopi cotton production declined.

Nampeyo

In 1895, the archaeologist J.W. Fewkes employed a group of Hopi men to help him excavate the ruin of Sikyatki, located near First Mesa and known for its beautiful polychrome pottery dating to the fifteenth and sixteenth centuries. One of the men was married to a woman named Nampeyo, born around 1860 in the First Mesa Hopi-Tewa village of Hano. Like her peers, the young Nampeyo learned to make pottery from older women. In the mid-nineteenth century, much Hopi pottery was influenced by Zuni styles, with a cracked white surface and decorations of representations of birds and flowers.

As the old Hopi pottery, with its bold forms and colors of red and brown on a yellow background, was excavated from the ancient ruin, Nampeyo began to incorporate the ancient designs in her own pottery. She originated a major revival of Hopi pottery that continues to this day. She also worked for the Fred Harvey Company promoting tourism in the Grand Canyon area and traveled to Chicago in 1910 to participate in the United States Land and Irrigation Exposition. From her home, the places she traveled, and a local trading post, Nampeyo sold thousands of ceramic vessels over the years, and many of her pieces ended up in museums. The quality and beauty of her pots soon became known throughout the world.

Despite her artistic recognition, Nampeyo's enduring significance was not yet generally understood upon her death in 1942. Many people regarded her work as particularly good specimens of the curious artifacts of a dying culture. It was only beginning in the 1970s that her true artistic significance gained general appreciation. Her descendants, and many of the people she inspired, have continued the tradition of fine Hopi pottery.

Today, many Hopi weavers use store-bought yarn and other materials, although many weavers have maintained traditional styles, forms, and functions. The classic dark-blue blanket is widely traded among the local pueblos and beyond, as are Hopi-embroidered cotton and wool blankets, belts, sashes, and kilts.

JEWELRY

Hopi crafters began to make silver jewelry in the late nineteenth century. Most of the early Hopi designs resembled the turquoise and coral work of the Navajo and Zuni artists from whom they learned their craft. Hopi silversmiths made small items, such as rings and bracelets, as well as larger items such as concho belts and necklaces. Non-Indians, such as those connected with the Museum of Northern Arizona, had an influence on the development of Hopi jewelry.

After World War II, some Hopi arranged for silversmithing classes to be paid for by the G.I. Bill. Contemporary Hopi silver work, characterized by a technique called silver overlay, dates from this period. This technique consists of oxidizing a piece of silver and then placing another piece of silver, with a design cut out of it, on top of the first piece. When the piece is buffed, it shines brightly, but the oxidized piece of silver below remains black, thus creating the intended effect.

Building on the veterans' classes, the Hopi Silvercraft Guild was formed in 1949, with Fred Kabotie as design director. People began to open individual jewelry shops in the 1960s. Most early Hopi jewelers were men, but today the art is practiced by men and women. Hopi silver is in high demand, and pieces by master Hopi silversmiths, such as Victor Coochwytewa and the late Charles Loloma, can sell for thousands of dollars.

KATSINA CARVING

Hopi men have long carved katsina dolls (*tihü*, pl. *tithü*). Traditionally, this activity took place in the kiva before a particular

Like the Zuni and the Navajo, the Hopi are also skilled in making silver jewelry. Hopi silversmiths are known for mixing contemporary and traditional methods and designs.

ceremony. Katsina dolls were given to girls and boys and used to teach children the names and purposes of the katsinam and, through them, the proper way to behave as a Hopi. As such, they were at least quasi-religious objects. Real katsina dolls are carved from cottonwood tree roots. They are then painted and decorated with cloth and feathers. Beginning in the 1880s, non-Native interest in katsinam began to influence their style and purpose, as they were increasingly made with an eye to the wishes of the collector.

All Hopi art (in fact, virtually all Indian art) has been subject to imitation and exploitation. Reasons range from economic necessity to sheer greed. Today, katsina dolls are part of a vigorous debate about how much of traditional culture to share with outsiders, when (formerly) sacred items are no longer sacred and may be displayed, and what to do when the work of both Hopi and non-Hopi crafters is culturally offensive. (One variation on this theme is the presence today of women carvers, something previously unimaginable. Another is the development of the "action-figure" katsina.) The Hopi Cultural Preservation Office is the official locus of many of these debates.

PAINTING

The Hopi probably first began to paint rooms and kivas in the 1300s. Kiva murals at Awatovi and other Hopi places include elements of Mesoamerican coloring and style and underscore the Hopi worldview of the interconnectedness of nature and humans. Modern Hopi painting dates from about 1900. In the 1930s, Fred Kabotie and others developed a distinctly Hopi modern style, and Hopi children began to have access to art instruction in school.

Today's Hopi painters address a wide number of styles and themes. One of Nampeyo's descendants, for instance—her great-great-grandson Dan Namingha—is a well-known Hopi painter. In 1973, he was also, with Fred Kabotie's son Michael and others, one of the founders of Artist Hopid, a group known for creating "secular paintings whose forms are based on ancient prototypes modified by contemporary art and whose subject matter is drawn from the mythical and oral historical traditions of the Hopi," as J.J. Brody wrote in *Hopi Kachina: Spirit of Life.* Artist Hopid also took as its central theme a pride in Hopi identity, values, and spirituality.

Contact with Outsiders

In the mid-sixteenth century, the Hopi people thought that an ancient prophecy had been fulfilled. Masauwu had instructed the people to watch for the return of Pahána, the Lost White Brother. This was a myth deeply ingrained in many Indian groups whose origins lay in what is now South and Central America. The Aztec, for instance, welcomed the Spanish conquistador Hernán Cortés as the incarnation of the white god Quetzalcoatl, and Cortés repaid their hospitality with mass murder and conquest. So it was that the Spanish came to Hopi as well.

In 1540, Francisco Vásquez de Coronado journeyed to what is now the American Southwest in search of the mythical seven golden cities of Cibola. He and his men found the peaceful Zuni, whom they proceeded to rape and plunder. Coronado then sent Pedro de Tovar to explore what was called the province of Tusayan to the north. Tovar took a Catholic priest with him. When the

Spanish arrived at Hopi, the Hopi made four lines of cornmeal, and the leader of the Bear Clan extended his hand palm up, knowing that Pahána would grasp it with his own hand palm down. Instead, thinking the Hopi were begging, the Spanish dropped a gift into the outstretched hand, and the Hopi knew that Pahána had not arrived after all. At this time, the major Hopi villages probably included Oraibi (Third Mesa), Shongopovi and Mishongnovi (Second Mesa), Walpi (First Mesa), and Awatovi (Antelope Mesa). Their precontact population—before a number of smallpox epidemics—is variously estimated to be in the vicinity of 30,000.

The first Hopi-Spanish encounter ended shortly thereafter, but within the following decades the Spanish conquered all of what is now the American Southwest. In 1598, Juan de Oñate demanded, and received, formal Hopi submission to Spain. Missionary activity began in 1629 at Awatovi, and by 1674 several missions had been established at Hopi. As was the case at other Spanish Indian missions, forced labor and torture, including violent punishment and child rape, were common. During this period, the Spanish also brought goods to Hopi from their global empire, including various cloths and metal items. Ill treatment by the Spanish led the Hopi to join the famous 1680 Pueblo Revolt, led by a Taos Pueblo man named Popé. The Indians of New Mexico tore down the churches and, killing hundreds, pushed the Spanish back into Mexico. The population of Hopi at this time—following roughly 140 years of European diseases, for which the Hopi had no immunities, as well as harsh treatment—was roughly 2,800.

ARRIVAL OF THE NAVAJO

Around the same time as the Spanish arrival, another group of people came to threaten the Hopi. This was an Indian group of Athabaskan origin, known today as Navajo. Unlike the settled Hopi, the Navajo were nomads, herding mainly sheep since the arrival of the Spanish and raiding the pueblos for livestock and slaves to sell to the Spanish. The Hopi welcomed these people and taught some to farm, but relations between the two groups soon soured. There was a big battle, which the Hopi won. Still, this peaceful people had been forced into two major conflicts. It was an ill omen of things to come.

Twelve years after the Pueblo Revolt, the Spanish returned to the Southwest. When they came to Hopi, the village of Oraibi did not allow them back, but other Hopi villages, including Awatovi, did. The Oraibi Hopi appealed to the Spanish for an end, or at least a reduction, of missionary activity, but the Spanish refused. As it happened, several of the most important clans in terms of Hopi ceremonialism lived at Awatovi, and the existence of missionary activity there thus threatened the entire Hopi society. In late 1700, just before the beginning of the annual ceremonial cycle, the Hopi village leaders took the extreme decision to eliminate Awatovi. All of the residents of the village, except women and girls who had not been baptized, were killed, and the village was physically destroyed. It would be more than 100 years until the Hopi were again threatened by missionaries. This act of mass murder and fratricide, however, weighed heavily upon the Hopi. Their self-image as a people of peace, a people living in harmony with all creation, had been damaged forever. Moreover, this was not to be the last self-generated convulsion for the Hopi people.

Other changes came to the Hopi following the destruction of Awatovi. Villages relocated to more defensive positions on the mesa tops. Tewa and other people, fleeing the Spanish, came to Hopi as refugees and were allowed to settle, establishing the villages of Hano and Payupki. From the Spanish, the Hopi acquired burros, sheep, and crops such as peaches. Among the other effects of the Spanish were an influx of horses, and with these the nomadic Navajo, as well as the Ute and the Apache, became masters of the Southwest and a growing threat to the Pueblo people. Despite the changes, the Hopi managed for almost 200 subsequent years, through strategies of active and passive resistance, to repel efforts to convert, exploit, and conquer them.

The Hopi living at Oraibi (*above*), one of the oldest and most important Hopi settlements, struggled to maintain their way of life as missionaries, disease, and government policies threatened their culture and existence.

NEW NEIGHBORS, THE AMERICANS

Generations passed, and a new nation, the United States, came into being to the east. In the early nineteenth century, trappers and explorers, the first of these "Americans," came to Hopi. Early relations between the two groups seemed pleasant until 1834, when an Anglo trapping party shot and killed 15 to 20 Hopi who were tending their gardens. In 1821, Mexico became an independent nation, and in the 1840s, the United States seized from Mexico what is now the American Southwest and California. Although the United States was founded on notions such as independence and property rights, it turned out that these ideals did not apply to some peoples living within (or even, for the most part, near to) their borders. The United States reserved the right to define those terms as suited it, and, in its view, the Treaty of Guadalupe Hidalgo, which ended the U.S.-Mexican War, rendered the Hopi subject to the United States. Thus did the Americans assert control over the Indian nations living within their increasingly vast country.

At first, the Hopi had reason to look with favor upon the United States. The first official Indian agent arrived at Hopi in 1864 and offered protection against the marauding Navajo as well as food (this was a period of drought and food shortage at Hopi) and clothing. Indeed, around the same time, the United States defeated the Navajo militarily, and in victory treated the Navajo people very harshly (this was the infamous "Long Walk," in which some 8,500 men, women, and children were forced to march roughly 300 miles, or 480 kilometers, to a desolate tract of land in eastern New Mexico). In an effort to secure Hopi assistance in their release from prison, the Navajo gave the Hopi their most sacred medicine bundles as a promise against future aggression. The Hopi accepted their promise and allowed some Navajo families to live on Hopi land (while helping the U.S. Army round up others), but, as we will see, history has revealed a relentless encroachment by the Navajo onto Hopi land.

The U.S. Bureau of Indian Affairs established a formal presence at Hopi by opening the Hopi Agency in 1869. In the 1870s, the long period of independence from foreign domination came to an end when the Mormons, the Moravians, and the Baptists all built churches at Hopi—the first foreign churches since the destruction of Awatovi—and the first trading post opened. Along with attempting to gain converts, the Mormons also began to take over a great deal of Hopi land. Around the same time, tourists, traders, and other outsiders began to come to Hopi in far greater numbers via newly completed rail lines. Between the trading posts, the distributions from U.S. Indian agents, and the influx of tourists, traditional Hopi material culture began to break down, replaced by non-indigenous farm tools, cloth, kerosene lamps, furniture, wagons, stoves, and food items. The change in material culture was reflected in other ways as well, such as in Hopi architecture, where doors in side walls began to replace traditional rooftop entrances.

In 1882, ostensibly in an effort to protect the Hopi against Navajo depredations, and certainly to help counter Mormon influence and to confine the Hopi to a defined area to facilitate non-Native migration into the area, the United States by executive order created a 3,863-square-mile (10,005-square-kilometer) Hopi reservation within the roughly 27,000-square-mile (70,000-square-kilometer) Navajo lands. (Actually, the order established the reservation for the "Moqui [sic] and such other Indians as the Secretary of the Interior may see fit to settle on." This ambiguity caused a great deal of pain and suffering among the Hopi and Navajo people.) At the time, several hundred Navajo were living on these lands. The reservation failed to include the growing Hopi settlement of Moenkopi. Five years later, in 1887, a boarding school opened at Keams Canyon. Other government schools at Hopi soon followed. Among other tasks, the Indian agents were charged with eradicating Indian culture inasmuch as it was in their power to do so. Their chief methods included discouraging traditional religious ceremonies, forcing children to attend non-Native schools, and encouraging conversion to Christianity.

DIVISIONS AMONG THE HOPI

Although a small number of Hopi had requested the school, most Hopi, and especially people living at Oraibi, were very resistant. Attempting to encourage them to enroll their children at the school, the U.S. government enforced a quota system of school attendance and invited several Hopi chiefs to travel to Washington. In 1890, the same year in which soldiers kidnapped more than 100 Hopi children and sent them to school, five chiefs made the trip. One of these chiefs, named Lololma, became a strong advocate for the new American way. His position exacerbated a major split within the Hopi people. The Friendly, or Progressive, faction favored cooperation with the United States and adaptation to the ways of the dominant society. This position was viewed with a great deal of suspicion by the Hostile, or Traditional, faction, which supported maintenance of the traditional Hopi way of life. Needless to say, the U.S. government aided the Friendly faction, even going so far as to arrest Hostile leaders and send 19 to Alcatraz prison in 1894 and 1895.

This split in Hopi society recalled the destruction of Awatovi and foreshadowed another cataclysmic event in Hopi history soon to come. As the split deepened, Lololma welcomed Mennonite missionaries, and in 1901 a Mennonite church was built at Oraibi, the Hopi's most conservative village. The leader of the "peaceful" Mennonites, however, devoted himself to exposing the secrets of Hopi ceremonialism. The success of his project played a significant role in further weakening Hopi society, which had been dealt a huge blow by a devastating smallpox epidemic in the early 1850s, when roughly two-thirds of the people perished, dropping the Hopi population to around 2,500. Lololma also encouraged people to move off of the mesas and to build American-style housing. Eventually a settlement of such houses, called Kykotsmovi (New Oraibi), grew up.

Meanwhile, beginning in 1879, non-Natives began to amass literally tons of Hopi property for their collections, either from the belief that Native people were headed for extinction and/or perhaps out of simple greed. With the ancient paths too difficult for the increased non-Native traffic, trails were widened to allow wagons to pass. In the 1880s, non-Hopi engaged in blasting to create even wider trails. Some of this blasting destroyed kivas

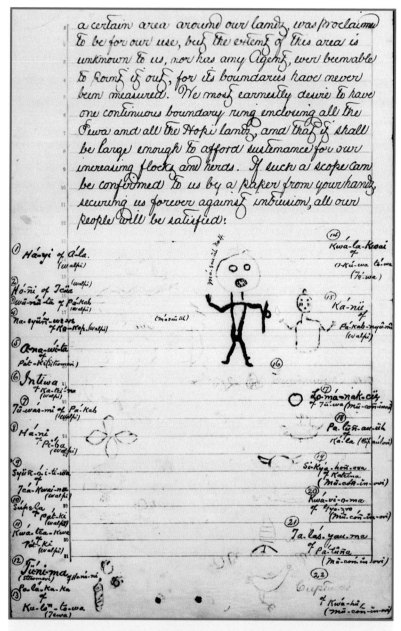

a certain area around our lands, was proclaimed
to be for our use, but the extent of this area is
unknown to us, nor has any Agent, ever beenable
to point it out, for its boundaries have never
been measured. We most earnestly desire to have
one continuous boundary ring enclosing all the
Tewa and all the Hopi lands, and that it shall
be large enough to afford sustenance for our
increasing flocks and herds. If such a scope can
be confirmed to us by a paper from your hands,
securing us forever against intrusion, all our
people will be satisfied:

In 1894, the Hopi issued a petition protesting the Dawes Act, a government policy designed to further weaken Native American tribes and nations by allotting tribal lands to individual male members of each household. This petition is signed with the symbol of every family in the tribe.

and other sacred sites. Around the same time, the first train tracks were laid in the area, making Hopi accessible to tourists. Passengers could disembark at either Holbrook or Winslow and make arrangements for a relatively brief trip to the Hopi mesas. Soon crowds of tourists, often organized by the Fred Harvey Company, began to attend the Snake Dance as one might attend a ballgame. This began the long process of commodifying—or exploiting for profit—Hopi arts, crafts, and religion. Besides tourists, the visitors included ethnologists and other social scientists, missionaries, souvenir hunters, and artists. All came because they wanted something from the Hopi people.

The U.S. government also wanted something from the Hopi people. In 1887, it passed the Indian General Allotment (Dawes) Act. The Dawes Act was meant to weaken and ultimately destroy Indian cultures by breaking up tribally held land (at Hopi, as we have seen, the land was clan-held, not individually owned). The act was a direct attack on the values, and the economies, of many Indian groups. The law provided that Indian land would be allotted to male heads of household, with any surplus deemed available for non-Indian settlement, thus supposedly liberating Indian people from collective ownership in favor of the free market. Roughly 90 million acres of "surplus" land were "liberated" from Indian people in this way. At Hopi, as at many Indian reservations, the idea that the government planned to give them, and at the same time attempt to control, their own land was as laughable as it was incomprehensible. Of course, the marginal Hopi land was particularly unsuitable for individual ownership and cultivation, and the Hopi actively resisted the allotment process, even tearing up the survey stakes. Allotment at Hopi was eventually abandoned but not before more damage was done to the Hopi social fabric and economy. In 1898, another smallpox epidemic struck.

At the dawn of the twentieth century, then, the Hopi, numbering about 1,900 people, were severely weakened by multiple assaults

(*continues on page 72*)

The Oraibi Split:
The Leaders' Testimony

Statement of Ta-wa-quap-te-wa, chief of Oraibi "Friendlies"
Department of the Interior, Indian School Service, Oraibi,
Ariz.

Sept. 16, 1906

I am the head man of this village. I am the head man of the
"friendlies" not of the "hostiles." I had nothing to do with
the "hostiles"; they had their own chief. The "hostiles" are
at a spring over north; they are there because they are not
friends to the white people; they were willing to leave their
homes. On the morning of the separation a crier called the
friendly people to meet at my house; I told the crier to do this;
I wanted the friendly people to drive the unfriendly people
away from the village [Oraibi]. The crier said nothing about
guns; they thought of them themselves and brought them
[the guns]. I did not tell the friendly Indians to use their guns;
when we were ready I said: "Come, let us go." I did not tell the
friendlies to fight with the "hostiles" and I did not tell them
not to fight. I went into the "hostiles's" room and said, "Are
you here?" I asked for Dan [Lomawuna]; a man pointed out
Dan; I said to Dan—"I told you one time to leave the village."
Dan is a Shu-pow-la-vi, lately from Shi-mo-pi-vi village; by
this I meant the people who had come over from Shu-pow-
la-vi and Shi-mo-pi-vi to Oraibi; I meant also the unfriendly
Oraibis who were in sympathy with them; we had agreed to
put all the "hostiles" out of the village. Our first intention was
to put the Shi-mo-pi-vis out; we did not agree on any thing
concerning the hostile Oraibis. The "friendlies" took hold of
Joshua and Dan, leaders of Shupowlavi and Shimo pivi; the
Oraibi "hostiles" helped the Shimo-pi-vi and Shu-pow-la-vi
hostiles. The "hostile" chief of Oraibi, Yu-ke-o-ma, said to me:

"No, I want these people to stay here." When the "hostile" Oraibis helped the Shi-mo-pi-vis, I told my people to put them all out. I saw no one that was badly hurt in the struggle. I told my people not to disturb the houses or property of the "hostiles."

I and my people watch the houses of the "hostiles" every night. The "hostiles" take care of their own crops. If any of the "hostile" Oraibis turn friendly I will take them back into my village. My people do not want to build a new village, but I do not wish to give an answer to that until I hear from Washington.

Statement of Yu-ke-o-ma, chief of the "hostiles" at Oraibi

Department of the Interior, Indian School Service, Oraibi, Ariz.

Sept. 16. 1906

I am the chief of these people ["hostiles"]. These people are friendly to the Government schools, but we do not want any schools. We do not want the Government to do with the children as they have been doing. These people have been in this camp about eight days; they lived at Oraibi before coming here. We left Oraibi because Ta-wa-quap-te-wa and his people drove us out. My people and Ta-wa-quap-te-wa's people have not been friendly for a long time; my people and Ta-wa-quap-te-wa's people quarreled first about the Government schools; Ta-wa-quap-te-wa's people wanted the Government schools, and my people did not want schools. My people and Ta-wa-quap-te-wa's people can live together in peace when his people agree to live the Hopi way. My people could never believe as Ta-wa-quap-te-wa's people believe, because we have talked about that for a long time and we have not agreed yet. We ["hostiles"] believe that the people who live the Hopi way are the ones who will have Oraibi, but

(continues)

(continued)

they ["friendlies"] have driven us out. My people do not want to make a new village.

Oraibi, Ariz, Sept. 16, 1906

Tawakwaptiwa. 9-16-1906: Oraiba Troubles, part I.
Yukiwma. 9-16-1906: Oraiba Troubles, part I.

Oraiba Troubles: Parts I–V, #88600-1909-Moqui-121. RG 75 Central Files.

Record Group 75: National Archives Record Group, Records of the Bureau of Indian Affairs, National Archives, Washington, D.C.

(continued from page 69)

on their way of life, including disease, Navajo encroachment, and increasing intrusion by the U.S. government, missionaries, tourists, and social scientists. In 1901, following the death of Lololma, the selection of a chief at Oraibi deepened the split in this most conservative village beyond repair. Clans and families divided, as each faction began to celebrate its own ceremonies. This, of course, was contrary to basic Hopi beliefs of harmony and proper social roles. Five years later, it appeared that another disaster like the destruction of Awatovi might be imminent. At the last moment, the Hopi were persuaded to draw upon their deepest beliefs and resolve the conflict nonviolently. The opposing chiefs, Tawáqwaptiwa of the Friendlies and Yukioma of the Hostiles, agreed to engage in a contest. The one to push the other over a line would be the winner; the other would leave Oraibi. Yukioma lost. Within hours, he and his followers—roughly half the population of the village—indeed departed Oraibi.

This was not the end of the dissension connected with the Oraibi split. Yukioma, guided by prophesy to bring his people along the route traveled by several of their clans during the migration periods, failed to do this, and instead founded the new village of Hotevilla, just eight miles (13 kilometers) from Oraibi. Federal troops arrived there soon after. They arrested the leaders of the split, sending some to jail in southern Arizona, some to the Carlisle Indian School in Pennsylvania, and some to a work crew in Keams Canyon. They also returned one group of people to Shongopovi, abducted 82 children and took them to a boarding school, and returned another group of people to Oraibi. The latter remained at Oraibi for roughly three years, after which they again left and founded the village of Bacavi. Oraibi's population was further depleted by migrations to the village of Moenkopi. Before the split, Oraibi had roughly 900 residents. In 1909 its population was 220. For his part, Tawáqwaptiwa spent the three years following the Oraibi split at the Sherman Institute in Riverside, California, courtesy of the U.S. government, learning how to become an even more effective "Friendly."

Modern Period

In the years following the Oraibi split, Hopi society continued to change, a result of the split as well as the growing pressures of the outside world. Tawáqwaptiwa, having returned from California in 1909, was bitter toward the United States. At his orders, more Christianized Hopi left Oraibi and formally founded Kykotsmovi, or New Oraibi. Others from this group went to Moenkopi, which itself soon underwent a split similar to that of Oraibi: More conservative people lived in Lower Moenkopi, while the Friendlies, or Progressives, lived in Upper Moenkopi. Slowly but steadily ceremonialism in Oraibi began to break down. By the 1930s, Oraibi held barely more than 100 people and its once-proud traditions were all but forgotten. Hotevilla, despite its own split in 1906, had become the home of Hopi traditional life. In 1929, Yukioma died and his son, Dan Qöchhongva, was recognized as the village leader.

Hopi children were sent, often against their families' wishes, to a boarding school on the reservation or to the Keams Canyon school. There, they were forbidden to speak their native language or practice traditional customs, leading many children to forget the Hopi way of life.

By 1910, four day schools and one boarding school were located on the Hopi reservation. In 1911, the local Indian agent, a man named Leo Crane, called in federal troops to forcibly remove Hotevilla's and Shongopovi's school-age children to the Keams Canyon boarding school. The pueblos at this time were in fairly desperate condition. Many of the children were ill and had few clothes, and, despite the opposition of the Hopi leadership, the agent might have thought he was acting in their interests. However, boarding schools were well known for their attempts to destroy Indian cultures by methods that included harsh punishment for using the native language and for any behavior regarded as "Indian." During these years the government routinely kidnapped children—and sometimes adults—and forced them to attend such institutions. In many cases, Indian children, made to feel ashamed of their rich cultures, forgot or failed to learn their native language and customs.

Forced attendance at schools was a major method, but hardly the only one, used to pressure the Hopi (and other Indian) people to abandon their traditions and take up the ways of non-Native society. Traditional religious ceremonies were outlawed. Traditional economic activities were disrupted—in many instances made impossible—resulting in many Indian people becoming despondent and economically dependent. At Hopi, the government, by way of its Indian agencies at Keams Canyon and Tuba City, provided some wage work in farming, construction, service at the agencies, and general manual labor. It also began to license traders to operate at Hopi, which in turn brought Hopi people more deeply into the cash economy and created a desire for foreign goods. These strategies had the dual effect of undermining the Hopi economy and encouraging people to move closer to the agencies, where traditions were weaker, thereby further disrupting village ceremonial and social life.

During this time, the federal government brought modern medical facilities to Hopi. Although this undermined traditional practices—in this case, healing methods—it also helped bring chronic medical problems among the Hopi under control and set the stage for a steady increase in population. Moreover, while government action had a major impact on Hopi life at this time, it was not the only force to be reckoned with. Churches expanded their activities, building more missions at and near Hopi and pressuring the people to reject their religious traditions and embrace Christianity. The non-Native economy, based primarily on farming, ranching, and mining, grew steadily, helped by the completion of the transcontinental railroad, which brought increasing numbers of non-Natives into closer proximity to the Hopi people. Arizona became a state in 1912, adding yet another layer of government activity to the mix. As cities grew, their businesses offered jobs, or at least the hope of jobs, to local Indians.

In the mid-nineteenth century, the Hopi had become aware of U.S. authority in the shape of the military forces and the official Indian agent, both of which played an increasingly prominent role in the people's lives. In the mid-1930s, the United States acted again to assert control over the Hopi and other Indian groups. For years, U.S. treatment of Native Americans within its borders had been largely characterized by military conquest, land grabs, destruction of traditional economic, social, and religious structures, and strong pressure to assimilate. The result was that by the 1920s, most Indian groups in the United States were poor, unhealthy, and demoralized. The shocking condition of these people was summarized in the 1928 Meriam Report. When Franklin Roosevelt was elected president of the United States in 1932, the reformers he brought into his administration were poised to act.

INDIAN REORGANIZATION ACT

One reform of Roosevelt's New Deal was the Indian Reorganization (Wheeler Howard) Act (IRA), a major component of the "Indian New Deal." Spearheaded by Commissioner of Indian Affairs John Collier, and passed by Congress in 1934, the IRA was intended to remedy past abuses, preserve Indian cultures, and allow Indian groups to "progress" by the method of "self-government." In short, among other provisions (such as ending the Dawes Act, returning some "surplus" Indian land taken under the allotment system, and providing funds for educational and other forms of assistance), the tribes could vote to accept the IRA and create U.S.-style constitutions and governments; in return, the United States would recognize those governments and accord those tribes certain rights. For some tribes, the IRA led to political stability and economic revitalization. For others it led to increased discord, as the new tribal governments, often sympathetic to the United States, clashed with more traditional elements. Some tribes, including the Navajo, did not adopt the IRA at all.

Among the Hopi, the four most traditional villages—Old Oraibi, Hotevilla, Shongopovi, and Mishongnovi—quickly condemned the IRA as another effort to undermine their culture and sovereignty and especially as completely alien to their traditional social and political structures. Kykotsmovi and Walpi, which was located near the agency at Keams Canyon, supported it. The other villages were divided. When the vote was taken in October 1936, roughly 86 percent of the vote was affirmative, but since the vast majority of Hopi chose not to vote at all in a typical sign of rejection, this was only roughly 15 percent of the Hopi people. Despite affirmation by such a small minority, the United States declared the vote a success. John Collier selected a non-Native anthropologist named Oliver La Farge to write the Hopi constitution and bylaws. The Tribal Council was established. Immediately the villages contested for power, exacerbating village rivalries. All members of the council were people from the "Friendly" faction; the traditionalists boycotted it altogether on the grounds that it was antithetical to Hopi traditions and a puppet of the U.S. government.

The Navajo, despite the promises made over their sacred bundles in the 1860s, steadily intruded onto Hopi land. By the early twentieth century the Hopi people were, for all intents and purposes, confined to roughly one-fifth of their land due to the trespasses of Navajo sheepherders. Although the United States had established the Hopi reservation in part to protect the Hopi from Navajo encroachment, it effectively reneged on that promise. The proximate cause was the issue of stock reduction. In the 1930s, the government, having concluded that the land could not support so many animals, moved to eliminate some of the more than 1.5 million Navajo sheep and goats. As a first step it divided the Navajo and Hopi reservations into 18 grazing districts. In 1936, it granted the Hopi exclusive use of District 6, which consisted of roughly 500,000 acres and all principal villages except Moenkopi.

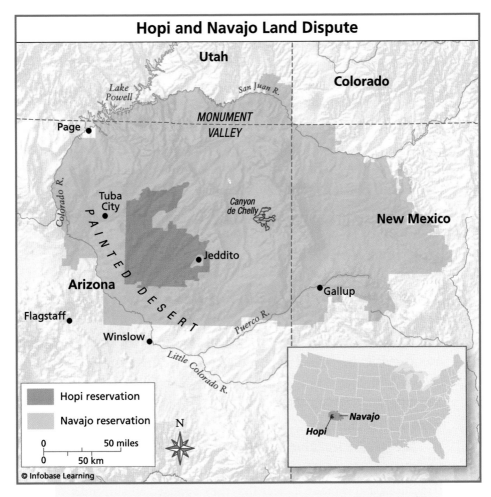

Hopi and Navajo Land Dispute

Navajo lands completely surround the Hopi reservation, leading to disagreements and fights between the two groups. The initial borders of the Hopi reservation formed a perfect rectangle, but deals and disputes have taken land away from the Hopi.

By doing so, the government granted de facto recognition of the Navajo takeover of three-quarters of the Hopi reservation.

WORLD WAR II

As was the case with many Indian tribes, World War II had a strong effect on the Hopi. Some served in the armed forces, significantly broadening the horizons of veterans who returned home.

Some registered as conscientious objectors, and still others—men and women—took advantage of war-related employment in cities such as Albuquerque and Los Angeles. These people often retained strong ties to their home villages, and many eventually returned, although some did not. Many Hopi people who were exposed to the outside world for the first time were not impressed. For instance, racial prejudice, the competitive ethos (directly opposed to the traditional value of cooperation), and compartmentalized religion (generally a "Sunday" matter, while for most Hopi, religion was practiced "24/7") were alien, and uncomfortable, to most Hopi people. On the other hand, some Hopi veterans were attracted by material values and objects, which made for friction when they returned to more conservative villages. Others were not attracted by material values but were convinced that the capitalist economy could help their people. When their more traditional elders rejected these notions, they felt frustrated and wondered if they could accept the continued leadership of the elders. At the same time many elders, unsure of what to make of the returning veterans with their new ideas, despaired of the survival of Hopi culture.

In 1948, the Traditional faction, bowing to the realities of contemporary politics, formally constituted themselves as the Hopi Traditionals and made it clear that they opposed all surrender of Hopi sovereignty. Indeed, in 1949 this group set out their beliefs in a letter to President Harry Truman that based their objections on a political ideology born of ancient myth and legend. In 1950, the Tribal Council, which had disbanded in 1943 after losing all popular support, re-formed with an explicit agenda of accommodation with the U.S. government; it received federal recognition in 1955. Both strategies—the council's cooperation and the Traditionals' resistance—were meant in their ways to perpetuate the survival of the Hopi people in the contemporary period.

In 1950, the Navajo-Hopi Long-Range Rehabilitation Act (NHLRRA) launched federal spending of tens of millions of

Letter to the President

A letter dated March 28, 1949, was sent by the Hopi Indian Empire in Oraibi, Arizona, to President Harry Truman. The letter read:

To the President:

We, the hereditary Hopi Chieftains of the Hopi Pueblos of Hotevilla, Shungopovy, and Mushongnovi humbly request a word with you.

Thoroughly acquainted with the wisdom and knowledge of our traditional form of government and our religious principles, sacredly authorized and entrusted to speak, act, and to execute our duties and obligations for all the common people throughout this land of the Hopi Empire, in accordance with the fundamental principles of life, which were laid down for us by our Great Spirit Masau'u and by our forefathers, we hereby assembled in the Hopi Pueblo of Shungopovy on March 9, 13, 26, and 28 of this year 1949 for the purpose of making known to the government of the United States and others in this land that the Hopi Empire is still in existence, its traditional path unbroken and its religious order intact and practiced, and the Stone Tablets, upon which are written the boundaries of the Hopi Empire, are still in the hands of the Chiefs of Oraibi and Hotevilla Pueblos. . . .

This land is a sacred home of the Hopi people and all the Indian Race in this land. It was given to the Hopi people the task to guard this land not by force of arms, not by killing, not by confiscating of properties of others, but by humble prayers, by obedience to our traditional and religious instructions and by being faithful to our Great Spirit Masau'u. We are still a sovereign nation. Our flag still flies throughout

(continues)

(continued)

our land (our ancient ruins). We have never abandoned our sovereignty to any foreign power or nation. . . .

Today we are being asked to file our land claims in the Land Claims Commission in Washington, D.C. We as hereditary Chieftains of the Hopi Tribe, can not and will not file any claims according to the provisions set up by Land Claims Commission because we have never been consulted in regards to setting up these provisions. Besides we have already laid claim to this whole western hemisphere long before Columbus's great, great grandmother was born. We will not ask a white man, who came to us recently, for a piece of land that is already ours. We think that white people should be thinking about asking for a permit to build their homes upon our land.

Neither will we lease any part of our land for oil development at this time. This land is not for leasing or for sale. This is our sacred soil. Our true brother has not yet arrived. Any prospecting, drilling and leasing on our land that is being done now is without our knowledge and consent. We will not be held responsible for it.

We have been told that there is $90,000,000 being appropriated by the Indian Bureau for the Hopi and Navajo Indians. We have heard of other large appropriations before but where all that money goes we have never been able to find out. We are still poor, even poorer because of the reduction of our land, stock, farms, and it seems as though the Indian Bureau or whoever is planning new lives for us now is ready to reduce us, the Hopi people, under this new plan. Why, we do not need all that money, and we do not ask for it. . . .

dollars to improve the reservations' infrastructure. Among the projects funded by the act were roads, a post office, telephone service, an airstrip, and new buildings. The NHLRRA also opened the

Now we cannot understand why since its establishment the government of the United States has taken over everything we owned either by force, bribery, trickery, and sometimes by reckless killing, making himself very rich, and after all these years of neglect of the American Indians have the courage today in announcing to the world a plan which will "convert the country's 400,000 Indians into 'full, tax-paying citizens' under state jurisdiction." Are you ever going to be satisfied with all the wealth you have now because of us, the Indians? . . . Have the American people, white people, forgotten the treaties with the Indians, your duties and obligations as guardians?

. . . We believe these to be truths and from our hearts and for these reasons we, Hopi Chieftains, urge you to give these thoughts your most earnest considerations. And after a thorough and careful consideration we want to hear from you at your earliest convenience. This is our sacred duty to our people. We are,

Sincerely yours,
Chief Talahaftewa, Village Chief, Bear Clan, Shungopovy
Basevaya, Adviser, Katchin Clan, Shungopovy
Andrew Hermequaftewa, Adviser, Blue Bird Clan, Shungopovy
Chief Sackmasa, Village Crier, Coyote Clan, Mushongnovi
Chief James Pongyayawma, Village Chief, Kokop Clan (Fire), Hotevilla
Chief Dan Katchongva, Adviser, Co-ruler, Sun Clan, Hotevilla

("Interpreters" and "Others" omitted)

Colorado River Reservation in western Arizona to Hopi colonists. Extensive road-building in the 1960s, paid for in part by "Great Society" programs such as the Office of Economic Opportunity,

greatly increased Hopi mobility and also facilitated modern housing and the construction of village suburbs. As modern life called,
many Hopi people left traditional villages for good, returning only
for ceremonial observances. Also at this time many Hopi people
began to tend livestock in addition to their farmlands.

Notably, many NHLRRA funds were allocated with an eye
toward encouraging non-Native companies to locate near the reservation and possibly provide jobs for Hopi people, rather than
encouraging local, Hopi-owned business activities. This was no
coincidence, for following the progressive period symbolized by
the "Indian New Deal," the forces of reaction set in. Claiming that
Indian people would be better off with the "smaller government"
they advocated, Republicans formulated a new Indian policy
known as "Termination," which would take full effect in the Eisen-
hower administration in the 1950s. The idea here was that Indian
tribes should become economically self-sufficient and fully independent—that is, terminated or separated from the "trust relationship" with the U.S. government that is enshrined in virtually all
treaties with Indian nations and was also settled U.S. law. A discussion of the Termination policy is beyond the scope of this book,
but suffice it to say that, like the Dawes Act, it was a fiasco for those
tribes it touched. Among its elements was a relocation service
program (established in 1948) that provided incentives for Indian
people to leave the reservation and resettle in the nation's cities.

ISSUES WITH THE NAVAJO

Beginning in 1868, the Navajo land base was extended several
times, officially by congressional and/or presidential action, and
unofficially via encroachment. Most of this expansion came at the
expense of land the Hopi considered to be theirs. In 1960, the Hopi
Tribal Council filed suit to recover their land from Navajo encroach-
ments. One crucial point of contention was the issue of which tribe
could prove prior occupancy of the land. The physical manifesta-
tions of ancient Hopi occupancy were, of course, etched in stone all
over the land, in the form of pictographs and petroglyphs, yet the

meaning of these symbols could only be revealed by Hopi traditionalists, who were boycotting the lawsuit on the ground that their lands were given to them by Masauwu, not the U.S. government.

Thousands of Native Americans volunteered to serve in the armed forces during World War II, including the Hopi. When they returned, however, their exposure to outside culture sometimes clashed with the traditional views on the reservation.

Another issue was land use. For the Hopi, land use was related to an ancient system of clan-based ceremonialism, and no one else had any right to tell them how to use their land. In the eyes of the Navajo, and those of most Americans, the Hopi, in farming a small part of their land, were making very little use of their resources, while the Navajo, through grazing, were making very good use of theirs. In a 1962 decision, known as *Healing v. Jones,* the U.S. Supreme Court ruled that the Hopi had exclusive rights only to District 6 and that the rest of the Hopi reservation would be considered a Joint-Use Area (JUA) to be shared between the Hopi and the Navajo. Given the size of the Navajo Nation, and the size of its herds, this decision essentially meant that the Navajo had exclusive use of the JUA. The decision was promptly appealed and led to extensive, and expensive, lobbying and litigation.

As important and as complicated as the issues relating to animal husbandry were, joint use pertained to more than grazing. With the rapid decline of Hopi isolation and the increasing role of the federal government in Hopi life, traditional economic activity declined with traditional ceremonialism. By the mid-twentieth century, subsistence agriculture had been more or less replaced by a cash economy, except that the Hopi people had very little cash. In 1961, the secretary of the interior authorized the Hopi Tribal Council to lease Hopi lands for the purposes of economic development. The council quickly secured leases for the exploitation of natural resources such as oil, timber, and minerals. With the roughly $3 million it earned from the sale of these leases, the council paid for attorney fees as well as a headquarters and compensation for its members. It also invested in a B.V.D company underwear factory. This venture ultimately failed, and the factory closed in 1975. Moreover, with its own funds as well as grants from the U.S. government, the council in 1970 opened the Hopi Cultural Center motel/museum complex, which features displays of Hopi arts and crafts.

COAL COUNTRY

Of all the mineral leases signed by the Tribal Council, the most significant was the one in collaboration with the Navajo tribe that allowed the Peabody Coal Company to strip-mine 400 million tons of coal on 65,000 acres of jointly managed land in the JUA. The deal also called for Peabody to pump 38 billion gallons of water from the aquifer for its slurry operations (that is, crushing the coal, mixing it with water, and transporting it via pipeline). Coal from these operations was meant to power electric plants in the Four Corners area. Strip-mining of Black Mesa began in 1968. This arrangement was, and remains, highly controversial. While it provided millions of dollars to the Tribal Council, it also severely damaged the local ecosystem above and below the ground. The decision to sign the leases was made unilaterally by the council, most of which was Mormon, with no open hearings or community meetings. Finally, the man behind the leases was John Boyden, the Tribal Council's Mormon lawyer who had also secretly represented Peabody Coal from 1964 to 1971. (Indeed, Boyden was the force behind the reestablishment of the Tribal Council in the 1950s; he needed an official body that could represent the tribe, legally if not in fact.) Boyden sold the tribe's coal rights for a fraction of what they were worth, especially considering the interests that stood to gain by the explosive growth of cities like Phoenix and Las Vegas that the coal plants made possible. As for the water rights, it is unclear whether the Hopi tribe actually signed a lease ceding these to Peabody Coal.

In 1971, the Hopi Traditionals filed suit to block the mining operations. In addition to technical claims about whether a quorum had been present when the lease was signed, the heart of the group's opposition was that the strip mine violated the most sacred elements of traditional Hopi religion, culture, and way of life. Although this suit was unsuccessful, some Hopi Indians continued the fight, sometimes in collaboration with outside groups, for decades thereafter.

While its mineral leasing partnership with the Navajo Nation garnered a great deal of money, relations between the two tribes remained tense over land use issues. In 1974, in an effort to resolve all such outstanding issues, the U.S. Congress enacted Public Law 93–531, known as the Navajo and Hopi Land Settlement Act (NHLSA), mandating that each tribe had the right to half of the JUA. The two tribes were charged with negotiating the boundary. When negotiations failed, a federal judge ruled that the Navajo would have to cede 900,000 acres of land and that several thousand Navajo and about 100 Hopi were to relocate within the new boundaries. In addition, yet another stock reduction program was instituted in an effort to save the land from desertification. This "solution," which led to years of further conflict, pleased no one. The NHLSA was largely written by John Boyden.

The Hopi Today

Issues concerning land use and ongoing conflict with the Navajo, along with continued cultural negotiation, have marked life among the Hopi people since the mid-1970s. As mentioned in the previous chapter, strip-mining for coal on Black Mesa began in 1968. There are two mines on Black Mesa, both owned by Peabody Coal. The Black Mesa coal mine serviced the Mohave generating station, near Laughlin, Nevada, via a 273-mile-long (439-kilometer-long) pipeline. The larger Kayenta mine, also on Black Mesa, supplies the Navajo generating station. Power from these plants provided electricity to Los Angeles, Las Vegas, Phoenix, and other cities in the Southwest for roughly 30 years.

Because the initial leases were so exploitative, in 1982 the Hopi Tribe levied a fee on all coal mined from Black Mesa, in part to benefit future generations. The fee, however, was vetoed by the assistant secretary of the interior for Indian affairs. When the Hopi worked out another structure for the fee, Washington again

Peabody Coal gave the Hopi millions of dollars in order to mine coal in Black Mesa. With the decline of coal mining on the Hopi reservation, tribal leaders must find different sources of revenue.

stepped in to protect Peabody Coal. (The tribal chairman at the time, Ivan Sidney, refused to press the government on this issue, at least in part because he may have feared a return to the Termination policies of the 1950s and 1960s. While the Hopi—and most other Indian tribes—desire the level of political sovereignty they once enjoyed, they understand that as long as this is not possible, the federal government must live up to its treaty obligations, gained by the Indians in consideration of the roughly 98 percent of their land that today is in the hands of the United States of America.) By 1987, the Tribal Council had renegotiated the leases on more favorable terms.

Peabody transported coal from the Black Mesa mine via slurry. Each ton of coal mined required 270 gallons (1,022 liters) of water—that's roughly 1.4 billion gallons (5.3 billion liters) per year to transport 5 million tons of coal to the generating station. Evidence suggests that the slurry operations are responsible for a significant drop in the local water table and the failure of local springs and wells vital to Hopi agriculture. In 2005, the Hopi and Navajo tribes stopped the extraction of water from the Black Mesa aquifer. This, in conjunction with a federal Clean Air Act lawsuit, shut down the Mohave generating station. This in turn resulted in the shutdown of the Black Mesa mine; its last day of operation was December 31, 2005. A new permit was issued in 2008, but in early 2010, an administrative judge revoked it.

With coal, natural gas, oil, and uranium resources, the Hopi Tribe is a member of the Council of Energy Resource Tribes (CERT). Founded in 1975, the council speaks with a unified Native American voice on mineral exploration and development policies and provides technical information to the member tribes. The Hopi Tribe is heavily dependent on income from its coal leases. The Navajo generating station provides it with about $11 million a year. The Black Mesa mine provided roughly $7 million a year in tribal income during its operation. In consideration of the royalties paid to the tribe, the Hopi people assume various direct and indirect costs of the mining operations, including environmental degradation and health problems. Besides the water issues, waste from the plant in the form of sulfur dioxide polluted the air around the Grand Canyon and Four Corners region for decades. Still, in 2009 the Hopi Tribal Council voted 12–0 to declare the Sierra Club and other environmental organizations persona non grata because of their opposition to the Black Mesa mines.

Despite the centuries-old animosity between the tribes, compounded by overgrazing issues in the nineteenth and twentieth centuries, many Hopi and Navajo people are convinced that their post-1960s conflicts have more to do with the politics of energy development, and particularly the intervention of Peabody Coal and state politicians, than any dispute between the two people per se. Lawsuits and confrontations continued into the 1980s and

1990s. The Big Mountain section of Black Mesa became an inter-
nationally known human rights flashpoint because of Navajo resistance to legally mandated relocations. In 1996, the two tribes agreed
on what was presumed to be a final settlement, in which roughly
250 Navajo families who did not wish to relocate would be offered
long-term leases, with the understanding that ultimate jurisdiction
of the land was in Hopi hands. However, although the Hopi have
regained a great deal of their land, their current land base is still
smaller than it was when the legal wrangling began. Moreover, as
some Navajo families continue to resist the settlement, the contro-
versy remains at least somewhat unresolved.

DEMOGRAPHIC FIGURES

In 2001, the Hopi Tribe's Enrollment Office reported a total population of 11,095. Between 75 and 80 percent of this population
lived in the Hopi area, and the official 2000 reservation population was 6,946 (that is, the reservation population, not all of whom
are Hopi, was 6,946, while the official tribal enrollment, not all of
whom live on the reservation, was 11,095). The median household income was roughly $23,000, which was approximately half
of the statewide median household income. In addition to roy-
alty payments from mineral development, the principal economic
activities involve federal and tribal programs. The Hopi Cultural
Center, located on Second Mesa, includes a restaurant, a motel,
craft shops, and a museum. Private-sector employment opportu-
nities include service stations, motels, restaurants, and arts and
crafts shops. Cattle production (for domestic use and the broader
beef market), tourism, small-scale farming and livestock grazing,
and construction also generate individual and tribal income.

In 2000, the Hopi Tribal Council created the Hopi Education
Endowment Fund to provide financial assistance to Hopi students. The tribe published the newspaper *Hopi Tutuveni,* written
in English and Hopi, until the Tribal Council shut it down in
December 2009, in a controversial decision that was likely taken
for political reasons. In 2001, KUYI, the first Hopi public radio

station, a project of the Hopi Foundation (http://www.hopifoundation.org), went on the air.

The Hopi Tribe is federally recognized, as is the Colorado River Indian Tribes, which is made up of members from the Mohave, Chemehuevi, Hopi, and Navajo tribes. There are 12 active Hopi villages. First Mesa villages are Sichomovi, Walpi, and Hano. Second Mesa villages are Shongopovi, Shipaulovi, and Mishongnovi. Third Mesa villages are Bacavi, Hotevilla, and Oraibi. Two villages, Polacca and Kykotsmovi, are located at the foot of First Mesa and Third Mesa respectively. Moenkopi (that is, Lower Moenkopi and Upper Moenkopi) stands about 50 miles (80 kilometers) to the west of Third Mesa, near Tuba City. The community of Winslow West is Hopi off-reservation trust land.

Today about 35 clans still exist, and about 40 extinct clans have interests that continue to be represented within the tribe. There are also roughly 14 or 15 religious societies. In recent decades the importance of traditional social structures such as clans has waned as nuclear families have become more significant. There are many reasons for this development, including pressures related to boarding schools and Christian proselytizing, the homogenizing tendency of modern American life, and indeed, intermarriage, primarily with other Indians such as the Navajo. One of the biggest reasons is the replacement of traditional economic structures with a cash economy, since cooperation among kin networks is less necessary in a cash economy.

Politically, *kikmongwis* (although not always from the Bear Clan) still lead individual villages. The Tribal Council, however, is the de facto (that is, it is the body officially recognized by the U.S. government) source of political power at Hopi. While there remains considerable opposition to that body (because of its checkered past and the fact that it does not represent at least one-quarter of the Hopi people), most Hopi understand that the Tribal Council is likely here to stay, and the main question is the extent to which it will promote, and operate within, an environment that is recognizably Hopi in some meaningful sense of the word. Today, the categories of "traditional" and "progressive" are somewhat fluid. Rather than two distinct sides, these words represent a continuum, and a person may well be "traditional" on some issues and "progressive" on others. Like so much about Indian cultures, it is best to look well below the surface before drawing conclusions.

It is important to note that all of these changes at Hopi were not the result of some inevitable unfolding of history. Colonialism may be defined as the political and economic control of one nation by another. In such cases, a dominant country usurps the sovereignty of a dependent nation and exploits its resources. This is a situation that defines the relationship between Hopi—and most Indian nations—and the United States. Since the mid- to late nineteenth century, the federal government has encouraged Christian missionaries to undermine traditional Hopi religion, attempted to apportion communally owned land to individuals and sell the "surplus" to non-Natives, created a "reservation" and then allowed most of that land to be taken by non-Hopis, forced (by means of its military) attendance at schools whose purpose was to destroy Native customs and traditions, virtually mandated the replacement of traditional political structures by a "tribal council," created an infrastructure that would facilitate resource extraction—coal mining—for the primary benefit of non-Hopis, and presided—by means of its agencies—over highly exploitative contracts regarding mineral extraction. The Hopi people, individually and collectively, have resisted and adapted in various ways, but nevertheless they have had to live within this colonialist situation.

CEREMONIALISM TODAY

Along with the secularization of much of Hopi political life, traditional ceremonialism has undergone significant change. As has been foretold in ancient prophesy, traditional religion has all but disappeared in Oraibi and other Third Mesa villages. The San Francisco Peaks, home of the katsinas, now are also home to several ski areas. Christian churches, especially Baptist, remain active at Hopi. When once everyone was initiated into one of the religious societies, today only some are initiated, and even for those people, such activities often conform to a nine-to-five work schedule. Some Hopi people, especially those who live farthest from the

Modern Hopi people are dedicated to maintaining the culture of their tribe. Participating in ceremonies, farming the land, and making crafts are some of the many ways they continue to honor the ancient traditions of their ancestors.

reservation, are only loosely, or not at all, connected to traditional beliefs, and as the elders pass away, aspects of the ancient knowledge pass with them.

Yet many aspects of Hopi ceremonialism remain alive and vibrant. The villages of First and Second Mesa, and especially Shongopovi, have retained the most robust ceremonial structure. Clan leaders and heads of religious societies still regulate ceremonies. Many Hopi observe a modified winter and summer ceremonial cycle, including Wuwutsim, some of the dances of the men's and women's societies, and some of the "social" dances. Corn remains at the heart of Hopi ceremonialism, as does the connection between corn, the sustenance of life, and the obligation to remember where the people came from and where they are going. Farming remains not only a subsistence activity but also a deeply religious one for many Hopi men. Some continue to farm clan land and give the produce to the household's eldest women.

VIBRANT ARTS

Today the arts thrive at Hopi, with a number of Hopi artists owning their own galleries and/or exhibiting at other venues. The Hopi people continue to make textiles, as they have done for centuries. Commercial art includes the making of katsina dolls, silver jewelry, woven baskets, and pottery (mainly at First Mesa). Cooperative marketing organizations and various enterprises for Hopi craftspeople, including Hopicrafts and Artist Hopid, are available on the reservation and off. Commoditization of katsina dolls continues unabated. Most such dolls at a typical Southwestern craft shop aren't made by the Hopi at all.

Hopi women continue the ancient art of basket making, especially on Second and Third Mesas. Girls today are instructed in basket weaving more often by their mothers or grandmothers than by a ceremonial godmother. Wicker basket weaving is especially prominent in the village of Hotevilla, where it is an important source of income for women. Some of the best wicker baskets are made by women in the seriously depopulated village of Oraibi.

Second Mesa is the center of coiled basketry. Nearly all the women in Shongopavi, Second Mesa's largest village, are members of one or both of the women's societies. On both mesas, younger weavers find inspiration and instruction in the older women, while older women whose weaving may have been interrupted while they raised their children find new stimulation by rejoining the group. Utilitarian items, especially burden baskets, are made less often, although some women still make baskets for piiki.

Paybacks, usually in the form of baskets, mainly plaques, occupy a good deal of some women's time. There are any number of reasons for a payback, including gifts (to newborn babies, winners of foot races) and wedding robes and associated gifts (such as food, shawls, and blankets) given by the groom's family to the bride's. All of these gifts incur social debt that must be repaid. Sometimes repaying debts associated with a wedding can take years. Quilting bees are a weekly activity at the mission churches and village community centers. Some of the most prominent Hopi women of the last century include the distinguished ceramist Otellie Loloma (1922–1992); the publisher and editor Rose Robinson (1932–1995); the poet Wendy Rose (1948–); the weaver Ramona Sakiestewa (1949–); and the artist and teacher Linda Lomahaftewa (1947–).

The theft and misuse of ceremonies and ceremonial objects is a major issue among the Hopi, as it is among many contemporary Indian groups. Looters regularly plunder Hopi sacred shrines and ancestral sites. Museums display sacred objects inappropriately. Even some Hopi attempt to sell their own sacred objects to non-Native collectors. The misuse and appropriation of ceremonial objects dates back to the nineteenth century, when tourists arrived to gawk at certain Hopi ceremonies. In recent decades, some people have begun to mock and/or misrepresent traditional ceremonialism and belief for profit, usually while claiming to "honor" Indian traditions. The Hopi have tried in various ways to preserve their privacy and retain, or reacquire, the items they need for their ceremonies. (There are several examples of successful repatriation of sacred objects. In 1958, the Fred Harvey Company returned five masks to the Hopi people; in 2001 after an extended negotiation, the altars from the Fred Harvey Company's Hopi House, located in the Grand Canyon, were repatriated.) The Hopi have banned tourists at certain ceremonies, and the Hopi Cultural Preservation Office has promulgated various protocols regarding research into things Hopi. The government has also helped, passing the Native American Graves Protection and Repatriation Act in 1990, although its enforcement remains uneven and its provisions complicated.

HEALTH, HOUSING, AND EDUCATION

Hopi Indians, as members of a federally recognized tribe, are entitled to health care as part of the Indian Health Service (IHS). The IHS Hopi Health Care Center, constructed in 2000, is located on the reservation. Various hospitals relatively nearby serve patients with more severe medical needs. The Hopi Substance Abuse Prevention Center opened in 2003. The Tribal Council has expanded the focus of its activities to attempting to address the host of social problems that have beset the Hopi people, including substance abuse, suicide, and child abuse. The Hopi held a number of mental health conferences in the early 1980s seeking to ground approaches to treating these scourges in traditional belief.

Housing preferences, which had begun to change rapidly after World War II, have markedly departed from the tradition. Although some of the old pueblos remain inhabited, the ideal that Hopi cosmology is embodied in the village and in housing styles, with the *kiva, sipapu,* and the absence of doors variously representing the creation and emergence myths, has largely given way to modern housing. Except at Walpi, where there is no electricity, Hopi houses are likely to include telephones, televisions, and satellite dishes. Moreover, the traditional model of houses built around the village plaza is also shifting to a more expanded layout.

In 1985, new Hopi schools were opened for all tribal students. Flexible schedules at the on-reservation schools allow students to

(continues on page 101)

Students at The Hopi School

Hopitutuqaiki—The Hopi School—(http://www.hopischool.net/) is located at Hotevilla. According to its mission statement, "The Hopi School is working to develop an educational process that is derived from Hopi rather than imposed from the outside." The school is "dedicated to developing an arts magnet school as an educational process for Hopi students, following the requirements of the federal and state governments for standards and accountability, but doing so through the arts, Hopi language and Hopi culture." The school's course offerings include quilting, pottery, weaving, photography, and glass blowing. Here are some recent student comments (used with permission):

• I had fun learning how to make a quilt which is used for baby naming ceremonies throughout Hopi. I learned what we use in the baby naming ceremony such as two perfect white ears of corn to protect the mother and the baby. I also realized that giving a quilt made on your own is very special. I learned how to cut material faster with a rotary cutter using a special mat.... The colors of my quilt are blue, light blue, and yellow with teddy bears on them.... I hope to continue making quilts as I learn and grow older. I was the youngest person in my class and I made two new friends and got to know special ladies who taught me how to quilt.

• The class reinforced my appreciation for weaving. Weaving allows me to express myself and my Native culture. I weave from my heart in hopes I and others will enjoy the good energy put into the textile.

• Raising questions about "art" as product/commodity. Specifically about katsina dolls. The fact that Mr. McGrath had some old, old pottery to show us takes us back in time. During the class, we wondered and talked about how the

(continues)

(continued)

ancient ones came about doing the pottery and what kind of tools they used and their techniques and ideas.

• I accomplished my goal by finishing my kilt. And another is to learn something from my Dad and to keep this weaving going as they are getting older. And also keeping something Hopi started and keep it going a[s] I get older.

• I liked the way everything was explained. All its meaning, values and the importance of Hopi weddings and the different types of weaving that are done in similar ways. And knowing your Hopi language gives you a better understanding of the Hopi life and meaning and values of weaving.

• I liked the class size, the instructor was patient and sharing of her knowledge of teaching and in both English and Hopi explained the ins and outs of putting the basket together. I particularly enjoyed learning Hopi vocabulary regarding the basket. The class as a whole, meeting people that have the same interest. I enjoyed the "act" of making an *yungyapu*. It was fun, confusing, and challenging. When I finished the yungyapu, I felt very proud, for me and the women in my family. Not being alone, enjoyed the laughter.

• This kind of basket is Hopi, and it commands its own vocabulary and is very much used for Hopi social life. I found that not much has changed since I was younger when I watched my grandmother make this basket. Learned the preparation of coloring reeds and the extra step that is put into it before being put to use. Only certain time of season materials are ready to be picked. And I believe it was more meaningful when instructions were given in Hopi. I learned new Hopi words and terminology in relation to making the plaques. (I am limited in the Hopi language). I wanted to know if I could be successful in the task. I enjoyed being with others in a "safe" learning environment. I want to know about being Hopi because I am Hopi. Still need more lessons.

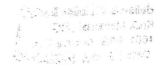

(*continued from page 98*)
attend village rituals and ceremonies. Children begin traditional education at about eight years old, with a series of initiation rites. The young are taught the Hopi way, composed of traditional principles and ethics and the value of kinship systems. Hopi High School opened in 1986 with an entirely local board of directors. The school emphasizes Hopi culture and language as well as computer technology.

IDENTITY AND THE FUTURE

Identity continues to be an important issue among the Hopi people. Efforts to preserve the native language are crucial to Hopi identity. Traditionally unwritten and untranslated, the strong Hopi oral tradition has preserved and passed down the language, and now Arizona State University has assisted in developing a Hopi writing system with a dictionary containing more than 30,000 words. Many Hopi today, including the younger generations, speak both Hopi and English. One area of debate is the question of how much Westernization or adaptation is acceptable and yet still allow one to "be" a Hopi. Should one allow modern conveniences (necessities?) such as electricity and running water into one's home? Should modern methods replace traditional dry farming? To what extent must the ceremonial calendar be maintained, and what should today's religious thought and practice be? There are many questions, and approaches, to the problem of modernity among the Hopi.

Today, Hopi families are disbursed, sometimes throughout the West and beyond. Many live in nontraditional housing and are full participants in the dominant society. For many Hopi, clans and religious traditions remain important, even vital, parts of their lives. Yet being Hopi involves not just, or necessarily, the old ceremonies but, for some, living with a Hopi consciousness. Indian people are no less "Indian" by having adapted to modern life than are non-Indians with old and even ancient histories and traditions. The Hopi survive by adaptation, as they have done for centuries and will continue to do.

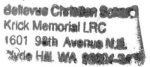

Chronology

ＹＹＹＹＹＹＹＹＹＹＹＹ

circa 10,000 B.C.	People lived in the area of Black Mesa at least as early as 10,000 B.C.
circa 2000 B.C.	Western Pueblo people probably begin to grow maize (corn) around this time.
0–A.D. 700	People living in the area of Hopi are part of a culture anthropologists call Basket maker. People live in caves and rock shelters and also in small villages, making baskets and pottery, among other items.

Timeline

circa 1100

The Hopi found the village of Oraibi on Black Mesa

1680

Pueblo Indians, including the Hopi, rise up and take back their territory from the Spanish

1887

Congress passes the Dawes Act

1600   **1850**

1540

Spanish soldiers, explorers, and missionaries enter Hopi

1700

The Hopi destroy the village of Awatovi to eliminate Spanish influence from their lives

1882

The United States establishes the Hopi (Moqui) reservation

700–900	This period is known to anthropologists as Pueblo I. The first villages on the Hopi mesas are established, and people slowly transition from pit houses to above-ground houses.
circa 1100	The Hopi found the village of Oraibi on Black Mesa.
900–1250	This period is known to anthropologists as Pueblo II and Pueblo III. People begin to build some multi-story houses, develop different types of pottery, and create more complex and diverse farming techniques.
1250–1500	This period is known to anthropologists as Pueblo IV. It is characterized by the development of highly specialized agriculture (including selective breeding and irrigation), mural and pottery painting, and mining.
1492	Christopher Columbus pilots his ships to land on the island of Hispañola in the Caribbean Sea.

1906

Intense Hopi factionalism leads the people to split the ancient village of Oraibi

1962

The *Healing v. Jones* court decision mandates joint use (with the Navajo) of most of the Hopi reservation, creating a formal Joint-Use Area (JUA)

1950   2000

1961

The U.S. secretary of the interior authorizes the Hopi Tribal Council to lease land for economic development

1974

The Navajo-Hopi Land Settlement Act leads to the partition of the 1.8-million acre JUA

1540	Spanish soldiers, explorers, and missionaries enter Hopi.
1598	The Hopi nominally submit to Spain.
1629	Missionary activity begins at the Hopi village of Awatovi.
1680	Pueblo Indians, including the Hopi, rise up and take back their territory from the Spanish.
1692	The Spanish reconquer Pueblo Indian lands.
1700	The Hopi destroy the village of Awatovi to eliminate Spanish influence from their lives.
1860	The Hopi artist Nampeyo is born.
1864	The first U.S. Indian agent arrives at Hopi.
1869	The first Bureau of Indian Affairs agency opens at Hopi.
1870s	The long period of relative Hopi isolation comes to an effective end in this decade, marked as it was by the arrival of relatively large numbers of Christian missionaries, tourists, and traders.
1882	The United States establishes the Hopi (Moqui) reservation by executive order.
1887	The U.S. Congress passes the Indian General Allotment Act, or Dawes Act.
1893	The U.S. government opens the Oraibi Day School.
1906	Intense Hopi factionalism, and/or perhaps the desire of Hopi leaders to fulfill an ancient prophesy, leads the people to split the ancient village of Oraibi, decreasing its population by roughly three-quarters. Several new villages result from this split.
1912	Arizona becomes a state.
1936	The Hopi Tribal Council is established.
1943	The Hopi Tribal Council is disbanded.
1950	The U.S. government passes the Navajo-Hopi Long-Range Rehabilitation Act. In the same year the Hopi Tribal Council is re-formed; it receives federal recognition in 1955.

1961	The U.S. secretary of the interior authorizes the Hopi Tribal Council to lease land for the purposes of economic development.
1962	The *Healing v. Jones* court decision mandates joint and undivided use (with the Navajo) of most of the Hopi reservation, creating a formal Joint-Use Area (JUA).
1966	The Hopi Tribal Council leases parts of Black Mesa to Peabody Coal.
1968	Peabody Coal begins to strip-mine coal on Black Mesa.
1970	The Hopi open the Hopi Cultural Center.
1974	The U.S. Congress passes Public Law 93–531, the Navajo-Hopi Land Settlement Act, which leads to the partition of the 1.8-million acre JUA and a generation of controversy over forced relocations.
1975	The Council of Energy Resource Tribes (CERT) is created, with the Hopi Tribe as a founding member.
1986	Hopi High School opens.

Glossary

amaranth   A grain native to the Americas and cultivated by aboriginal people as early as 3500 B.C.

anthropology   The branch of the social sciences concerned with the study of humanity.

archaeology   The study of the human past, primarily through material evidence such as artifacts and the environmental record.

arroyo   A ditch or a gully.

atlatl   A tool used to throw a projectile, such as a spear or a dart, with increased force, distance, and accuracy. Many ancient peoples used it in hunting.

check dams   Dams placed across small channels to slow water flow and control erosion.

clan   A group of people related by kinship or descent.

dibble   A pointed gardening tool used to make holes in the ground in preparation for planting.

G.I. Bill   A 1944 law that provided educational benefits for men and women returning from military service in World War II.

Great Society   The popular name of the progressive social welfare and civil rights legislation of the Lyndon Johnson administration.

Indian New Deal   Refers in general to John Collier's tenure as commissioner of the U.S. Bureau of Indian Affairs and specifically to the Indian Reorganization Act, which was designed to empower Indian groups to join in partnership with the federal government to carry out various programs.

Joint-Use Area (JUA)   The formal designation that was meant to settle the Hopi-Navajo land dispute.

katsina   In Hopi mythology and religion, spirits of all things.

kikmongwi   Traditional kinship-based leaders of Hopi villages.

kiva An underground chamber used by most Pueblo people for prayer, religious ceremony, and religious instruction.

lineage A group of people in direct line of descent. Groups of lineages combine to form clans, traditionally the basis of Hopi social organization.

mano A type of pestle, used with a metate to grind grain or seeds.

mesa A flat-topped mountain or hill, usually with steep sides.

metate A mortar, or stone, used in grinding grain and seeds.

Moqui or **Moki** The Hopi were long known to non-Native people by this name.

Pahána According to Hopi mythology, Masauwu instructed the people to watch for the return of *Pahána,* the Lost White Brother, who will come at the end of the Fourth World and usher in a new age.

páhos Sticks adorned with eagle feathers used in some Hopi ceremonies.

pictographs and petroglyphs Pictographs are drawings that convey meaning through symbols. Petroglyphs are rock carvings of symbols meant to convey certain meanings.

piiki A very thin wafer made out of blue corn finely ground with ash added.

repatriation The process of returning a sacred or culturally meaningful object to its original owners.

sipapu In Hopi mythology, the opening in the sky that led to successive worlds that the Hopi passed through.

strip mining A technique for mining coal and other minerals, characterized by the use of giant machines to scrape off the layer of earth to expose the mineral seams below.

Termination The informal name of U.S. Indian policy of the late 1940s into the 1960s that formed to "liberate" Indian people and tribes from "government control" by ending the historic trust relationship with the U.S. government that is guaranteed by numerous treaties, turning reservations into municipalities, and forcing the tribes to pay taxes on their "assets."

tithü Commonly known as *katsina* dolls, they are said to embody the spirit of the *katsina* they represent. They are traditionally given to children to help instruct them in what is considered proper behavior for a Hopi.

yucca A genus of shrubs and trees in the agave family. It has sword-like leaves and a large central cluster of white flowers.

Bibliography

Adams, E. Charles, and Kelley Ann Hays, eds. *Homol'ovi II: Archaeology of an Ancestral Hopi Village, Arizona.* Tucson: University of Arizona Press, 1991.

Beck, Peggy, and Anna Walters. *The Sacred: Ways of Knowledge, Sources of Life.* Tsaile, Ariz.: Navajo Community College Press, 1977.

Benedek, Emily. *The Wind Won't Know Me: A History of the Navajo-Hopi Land Dispute.* New York: Knopf, 1992.

Bernardini, Wesley. *Hopi Oral Tradition and the Archaeology of Identity.* Tucson: University of Arizona Press, 2005.

Boxberger, Daniel. *Native North Americans: An Ethnohistorical Approach.* Dubuque, Iowa: Kendall/Hunt Publishing, 1990.

Brugge, David. *The Navajo-Hopi Land Dispute: An American Tragedy.* Albuquerque: University of New Mexico Press, 1994.

Clemmer, Richard. *Roads in the Sky: The Hopi Indians in a Century of Change.* Boulder, Colo.: Westview Press, 1995.

Courlander, Harold. *Hopi Voices: Recollections, Traditions, and Narratives of the Hopi Indians.* Albuquerque: University of New Mexico Press, 1982.

Davis, Mary B., ed. *Native America in the Twentieth Century.* New York: Garland Publishing, 1994.

Dockstader, Frederick. *The Kachina and the White Man: The Influences of White Culture on the Hopi Kachina Cult.* Albuquerque: University of New Mexico Press, 1985.

Dutton, Bertha. *American Indians of the Southwest.* Albuquerque: University of New Mexico Press, 1983.

Gilbert, Matthew Sakiestewa. *Education Beyond the Mesas: Hopi Students at Sherman Institute, 1902–1929.* Lincoln: University of Nebraska Press, 2010.

Hackett, Charles Wilson, ed.. *Historical Documents Relating to New Mexico, Nueva Vizcaya, and Approaches Thereto, to 1773.* Washington: Carnegie Institution of Washington, 1937.

Kramer, Barbara. *Nampeyo and Her Pottery.* Albuquerque: University of New Mexico Press, 1996.

Loftin, John D. *Religion and Hopi Life in the Twentieth Century.* Bloomington: Indiana University Press, 1991.

Malotki, Ekkehart, ed. *Hopi Tales of Destruction.* Lincoln: University of Nebraska Press, 2002.

Ortiz, Alfonso, ed. *Handbook of North American Indians, Vol. 9 Southwest.* Washington, D.C.: Smithsonian Institution, 1983.

Page, Susanne and Jake. *Hopi.* New York: Harry N. Abrams, 1994.

Pearlstone, Zena. *Katsina: Commodified and Appropriated Images of Hopi Supernaturals.* Los Angeles: UCLA Fowler Museum of Cultural History, 2001.

Pritzker, Barry M. *Native Americans: An Encylcopedia of History, Culture, and Peoples.* Santa Barbara: ABC-CLIO, 1998.

Ricks, J. Brent, and Alexander E. Anthony Jr.. *Kachinas, Spirit Beings of the Hopi.* Albuquerque: Avanyu Publishing, 1993.

Rushforth, Scott, and Steadman Upham. *A Hopi Social History.* Austin: University of Texas Press, 1992.

Seaman, P. David, ed. *Born a Chief: The Nineteenth Century Hopi Boyhood of Edmund Nequatewa.* Tucson: University of Arizona Press, 1993.

Simmons, Leo, ed. *Sun Chief: The Autobiography of a Hopi Indian.* New Haven, Conn.: Yale University Press, 1942.

Teiwes, Helga. *Hopi Basket Weaving: Artistry in Natural Fibers.* Tucson: University of Arizona Press, 1996.

_____. *Kachina Dolls: The Art of Hopi Carvers.* Tucson: University of Arizona Press, 1991.

Thompson, Laura. *Culture in Crisis: A Study of the Hopi Indians.* New York: Harper and Brothers, 1950.

Thompson, Laura, and Alice Joseph. *The Hopi Way.* New York: Russell & Russell, 1965.

Titiev, Mischa. *The Hopi Indians of Old Oraibi: Change and Continuity.* Ann Arbor: University of Michigan, 1972.

Trimble, Stephen. *The People: Indians of the American Southwest.* Santa Fe: School of American Research Press, 1993.

Walker, Willard, and Lydia Wyckoff, eds. *Hopis, Tewas, and the American Road.* Albuquerque: University of New Mexico Press, 1983.

Washburn, Dorothy K. *Living in Balance: The Universe of the Hopi, Zuni, Navajo and Apache.* Philadelphia: University of Pennsylvania, 1995.

Washburn, Dorothy K., ed. *Hopi Kachina: Spirit of Life.* San Francisco: California Academy of Sciences, 1980.

Waters, Frank. *Book of the Hopi.* New York: Viking Press, 1963.

Whiteley, Peter. *Deliberate Acts: Changing Hopi Culture through the Oraibi Split.* Tucson: University of Arizona Press, 1988.

_____. *Rethinking Hopi Ethnography.* Washington: Smithsonian Institution Press, 1998.

Wood, John J. *"Sheep Is Life": An Assessment of Livestock Reduction in the Former Navajo-Hopi Joint Use Area.* Flagstaff, Ariz.: Northern Arizona University, 1982.

Wright, Margaret. *Hopi Silver.* Flagstaff, Ariz.: Northland Press, 1972.

Yava, Albert. *Big Falling Snow: A Tewa-Hopi Indian's Life and Times and the History and Traditions of His People.* Albuquerque: University of New Mexico Press, 1978.

Further Resources

Books

Kosik, Fran. *Native Roads: The Complete Motoring Gude to the Navajo and Hopi Nations.* Tucson, Ariz.: Rio Nuevo Publishers, 2005.

Kuyiyumptewa, Stewart B., Carolyn O'Bagy Davis, and the Hopi Cultural Preservation Office. *The Hopi People.* Mount Pleasant, S.C.: Arcadia Publishing, 2009.

Nequatewa, Edmund. *Truth of a Hopi: Stories Relating to the Origin, Myths, and Clan Histories of the Hopi.* Radford, Va.: Wilder Publishing, 2007.

Waters, Frank. *Pumpkin Seed Point: Being within the Hopi.* Athens: Ohio University Press, 1973.

Web Sites

"Black Mesa Water Coalition Stops Peabody Coal"
http://www.examiner.com/energy-policy-in-san-francisco/black-mesa-water-coalition-stops-peabody-coal
This article on the Black Mesa Water Coalition comes from the San Francisco Examiner.

"Censored News: Hopi and Navajo Stop Peabody Coal Mine Expansion"
http://bsnorrell.blogspot.com/2010/01/hopi-and-navajo-stop-peabody-coal-mine.html
Censored News *is an independent outlet for indigenous peoples and human rights news.*

Hopi Cultural Preservation Office
http://www.nau.edu/~hcpo-p/
The Hopi Cultural Preservation Office Web site provides a range of information about visiting the Hopi, conducting research, and teaching and

learning, as well a number of useful links to further information about the Hopi.

The Hopi Foundation
http://www.hopifoundation.org/
The Hopi Foundation, located in Kykotsmovi, Arizona, "exemplifies the Hopi teaching of 'Itam naapyani' or doing the work ourselves. Established by local Hopis, [it] promote[s] self sufficiency, proactive community participation in our own destiny, self reliance and local self determination."

The Hopi School
http://www.hopischool.net/
This is the official Web site of The Hopi School in Hotevilla, Arizona.

Hopi Tribal Courts
http://hopicourts.com/
The official Web site of the Hopi Tribal Courts provides a range of information about Hopi law and judicial issues.

Index of Native American Resources on the Internet
http://www.hanksville.org/NAresources
This index is maintained by Karen Strom.

Inter Tribal Council of Arizona: Hopi Tribe
http://www.itcaonline.com/tribes_hopi.html
The Inter Tribal Council of Arizona serves as a resource for Indian tribes in Arizona.

Land Use History of the Colorado Plateau: Hopi
http://cpluhna.nau.edu/People/hopi.htm
This Web site is a service of Northern Arizona University.

"Monitoring the Effects of Ground-Water Withdrawals from the N Aquifer in the Black Mesa Area, Northeastern Arizona"
http://pubs.usgs.gov/fs/FS-064–99/
This is a U.S. Geological Survey article about the effects on local groundwater of the slurry operation at Peabody Coal's Black Mesa mine.

Native Web

http://www.nativeweb.org/

Native Web "is an international, nonprofit, educational organization dedicated to using telecommunications including computer technology and the Internet to disseminate information from and about indigenous nations, peoples, and organizations around the world; to foster communication between Native and non-Native peoples; to conduct research involving indigenous peoples' usage of technology and the Internet; and to provide resources, mentoring, and services to facilitate indigenous peoples' use of this technology."

Navajo-Hopi Observer

http://navajohopiobserver.com

The Navajo-Hopi Observer *provides news for the Navajo and Hopi Nations and Winslow, Arizona.*

SourceWatch: Black Mesa Coal Mine

http://www.sourcewatch.org/index.php?title=Black_Mesa_coal_mine

This is an article on the Black Mesa coal mine by SourceWatch, *a publication of the Center for Media and Democracy.*

Techqua Ikachi: Land and Life, the Traditional Viewpoint

http://www.jnanadana.org/hopi/techqua_ikachi_i.html

Techqua Ikachi *purports to be published by traditional leaders in the village of Hotevilla.*

Films

Beyond the Mesas: A Film of the Hopi Boarding School Experience. DVD, directed by Allan Holzman, 2006, Santa Monica, California. Distributed by 716 Productions and Learning Who We Are, 2006. See http://beyondthemesas.com/.

Hopi Land. VHS, directed by Christopher McLeod, 2001, Berkeley, California. A production of the Sacred Land Film Project of Earth Island Institute. A presentation of the Independent Television Service in association with Native American Public Telecommunications with funding provided by the Corporation for Public Broadcasting. See http://www.bullfrogfilms.com/catalog/hopi.html.

Hopi Prophecy. DVD, New York, New York, Films Media Group, 1991. See http://ffh.films.com/id/7808/Hopi_Prophecy.htm.

Hopi, Songs of the Fourth World. DVD, directed by Pat Ferrero, 1985. Distributed by New Day Films, Harriman, New York. See http://www. newday.com/films/Hopi_Songs.html.

Itam Hakim, Hopiit. DVD, Victor Masayesva Jr., 1985. Produced by IS Productions, distributed by Electronic Arts Intermix, New York. See http://www.nativenetworks.si.edu/eng/orange/itam_hakim_hopiit. htm.

Picture Credits

Index

About the Contributors

BARRY PRITZKER has written *Native America Today: A Guide to Community Politics and Culture* and *Native Americans: An Encyclopedia of History, Culture and Peoples,* and has coedited the *Encyclopedia of American Indian History.* He has taught on the Taos Pueblo and at schools in Arizona, Massachusetts, and France. He currently works and occasionally teaches at Skidmore College.

Series editor **PAUL C. ROSIER** received his Ph.D. in American History from the University of Rochester in 1998. Dr. Rosier currently serves as Associate Professor of History at Villanova University (Villanova, Pennsylvania), where he teaches Native American History, American Environmental History, Global Environmental Justice Movements, History of American Capitalism, and World History.

In 2001, the University of Nebraska Press published his first book, *Rebirth of the Blackfeet Nation, 1912–1954;* in 2003, Greenwood Press published *Native American Issues* as part of its Contemporary Ethnic American Issues series. In 2006, he coedited an international volume called *Echoes from the Poisoned Well: Global Memories of Environmental Injustice.* Dr. Rosier has also published articles in the *American Indian Culture and Research Journal,* the *Journal of American Ethnic History,* and *The Journal of American History.* His *Journal of American History* article entitled "They Are Ancestral Homelands: Race, Place, and Politics in Cold War Native America, 1945–1961" was selected for inclusion in *The Ten Best History Essays of 2006–2007,* published by Palgrave MacMillan in 2008; and it won the Western History Association's 2007 Arrell Gibson Award for Best Essay on the history of Native Americans. His latest book, *Serving Their Country: American Indian Politics and Patriotism in the Twentieth Century* (Harvard University Press), is winner of the 2010 Labriola Center American Indian National Book Award.